A Casebook of Inclusive Pedagogical Practices for Second Language Teacher Education

A Casebook of Inclusive Pedagogical Practices for Second Language Teacher Education

Amy B. Gooden

UNIVERSITY OF MICHIGAN PRESS
ANN ARBOR

Published in the United States of America
The University of Michigan Press
Manufactured in the United States of America

Printed on acid-free paper

ISBN-13: 978-0-472-03793-3 (print)
ISBN-13: 978-0-472-12899-0 (ebook)

2024 2023 2022 2021 4 3 2 1

Contents

Introduction

The 21st century's multicultural and multilingual world has spurred the need for competent second language (L2) teachers in a range of K–12 and post-secondary contexts who understand the need to create an inclusive classroom. L2 teachers have the immense responsibility of equipping future global citizens with the gift of communication in another language so they can voice their needs and ideas across linguistic and cultural boundaries. As classrooms grow increasingly diverse in K–12 and post-secondary settings, teachers need to consider inclusive practices to meet the demands of a range of learners, including culturally and linguistically diverse students, learners with trauma and anxiety, SLIFE (students with limited or interrupted formal education), newcomers and refugees, heritage language learners, and students with cognitive and physical disabilities.

This casebook is designed to broaden L2 teacher knowledge, thinking, and practice with regard to making language and learning accessible to **all** students. Language teachers are especially accountable for promoting socially just, inclusive, decolonizing, and multicultural pedagogical practices and curricula; at this critical juncture in history, this book is intended to raise language teachers' awareness of the importance of critically examining and reflecting on the intersectionality of language education and inclusive pedagogical practices from what Waitoller and Thorius (2016) refer to as a "cross-pollinated perspective."

As presented in Gooden and Zlateva (2018), case-based pedagogy is an innovative sociocultural approach to second language teacher education (SLTE) that forces participants to grapple with exactly the kinds of dilemmas and decisions teachers confront every day. In doing so, it redefines the traditional educational dynamic in which the professor dispenses knowledge and students passively receive it. One key characteristic of case-based pedagogy is the case method, a teaching approach that consists of presenting students with a case that puts them in the role of a decision-maker facing a problem. In a case method classroom, the instructor and students are actively engaged in dissecting the information to explore the context, characters, issues, options, criteria, and solutions (Ellet, 2007).

With a cumulative experience of two decades teaching language using the case-based method at Harvard University and other universities, I have productively applied this approach in these settings:

- pre-service undergraduate and graduate ESL/TESOL/ Bilingual K–12 teacher licensure programs
- pre-service undergraduate and graduate Modern Foreign and World Language K–12 licensure programs
- in-service professional development workshops with teachers across content areas who are interested in supporting the language needs of diverse learners
- in-service professional development workshops for Modern Foreign and World Language teachers
- graduate TESOL education programs
- in-house faculty development in English for Academic Purposes (EAP) and intensive English programs

This *Casebook* offers written representations of actual language classroom and inclusive education dilemmas from private, charter, and public schools, and urban and suburban contexts. It also offers a range of language program designs at elementary, secondary, and tertiary levels: K–12 English as a second language (ESL)/bilingual education/sheltered English immersion (SEI); world language (WFL); and post-secondary EAP contexts.

This innovative casebook can be used successfully as a stand-alone text in the typical courses in language teacher preparation programs in schools of education but can also be used in other disciplines such as Disabilities Studies and Special Education courses, as well as general teacher preparation courses:

- Practicum or Student Teaching Seminars for language educators
- Methods of Teaching Modern Foreign or World Languages, TESOL, and Bilingual Education courses
- Issues in Bilingualism
- Language and Literacy
- Sociolinguistics and Education
- Applied Linguistics
- ESL and SEI Endorsement
- Intercultural Education
- Special Education and Disability Studies

The book can also be used as a supplementary text in any of these courses and as a resource in professional development programs for in-service language teachers in K–12 and post-secondary contexts.

Language teacher educators can use this text in their courses and workshops to build on and extend theoretical foundations, while making critical practical connections. All the cases are based on real-life dilemmas faced by practitioners in the field and have been informed by discussions with pre-service and in-service student teachers.

The 12 cases presented here cover a range of inclusive language teaching and learning issues that practitioners are likely to face in their respective teaching contexts. All the cases deal with hot topics and trending issues that will resonate with readers. Most of the cases reflect authentic situations in K–12, while a smaller number of post-secondary cases address key aspects of teaching academic English in the global higher education context. A primary selection criterion for the cases was alignment with national and state subject matter knowledge standards for language teachers. Even though all the names of schools and individuals are pseudonyms, in some of the cases, readers will notice references to specific state and local regulations and policies. Based on my teaching and research, I am confident that the issues in the cases present topics that are generalizable.

A Few Important Notes

One important point I would like to make clear: In some situations, readers may detect stereotypical thinking and implicit bias about culture, race, ethnicity, ability, and socioeconomic conditions in the case apparatus. This is a conscious decision because my experience with case discussions shows that including such perspectives and attitudes **generates critical analysis of the real issues in contemporary multicultural and multilingual contexts.** In the same vein, rather than fueling stereotypes, the provocative—and sometimes extreme—language in the narrative **is intended to hone sensitivity to the cross-cultural dimension of language teaching. It is imperative for the case facilitator to model inclusive teaching and establish ground rules for respectful, inclusive, and meaningful conversations as part of the initial introduction to case learning and as part of the pre-case discussion orientation process.**

In the spirit of the Harvard Business School case structure, **the cases here are NOT intended as exemplars of practice to be emulated or illustrations of existing theories**; instead, they are **problem-based narratives** that resist clear-cut answers or solutions and remain open ended to stimulate further investigation and reflection. The narrative style is **purposefully neutral** and, at times, deliberately includes seemingly irrelevant information or redundant detail that serve as distractors from the core issues. The goal is to **mimic the complexity of the classroom** where teachers confront a range of pedagogical and learning challenges, and the ensuing experience is one of being steeped like a teabag in a hot cup of reality where critical, real-time decisions depend on keen professional discernment.

The cases are accompanied by pre- and post-problem sets and in-class discussion questions. Each case is designed to promote specific language learning and teaching goals. Broadly defined, learning with cases involves an instructional and curricular blend of individual reflection and group analysis of authentic cases.

Even though the use of the case method does not presuppose familiarity with key theoretical underpinnings in linguistics or second language education methods, I would encourage participants with limited formative training in these subjects to consult the recommended readings that accompany the Commentary before reading each case. This will ensure richer and more informed discussion and analysis of the issues in the case.

The Commentary (available online) provided for each case outlines the specific objectives of each case and is designed to assist professors, professional development leaders, as well as anyone who teaches with the *Casebook for Second Language Teacher Education* (Gooden & Zlateva, 2018). The Commentary features:

- additional background information on the case
- overarching implications of the case in terms of teacher knowledge, praxis, and thinking
- specified language teaching and learning outcomes
- suggestions for best-practice instruction

Overall Structure of the Book

The case chapters are organized as follows:

Chapter 2 includes Elementary Inclusive ESL/SEI/Bilingual Education cases with accompanying discussion questions and problem sets.

Chapter 3 covers Secondary Inclusive ESL/SEI/TESOL cases with accompanying discussion questions and problem sets.

Chapter 4 includes Inclusive World Language Education cases with accompanying discussion questions and problem sets.

Chapter 5 presents Inclusive Post-Secondary English for Academic Purposes cases with accompanying discussion questions and problem sets.

Table I.1 charts the primary pedagogical issues of each case for quick reference and to allow users to find a synthesis of the issues and objectives by case or setting. For highlights of other issues, teachers may refer to the online Commentary.

Table I.1
Chart of Cases and Pedagogies

Case	Language Teaching Objectives	Inclusive Teaching Objectives
	Inclusive Elementary	
Mountain Ridge Elementary School	▪ Support students' development of Basic Interpersonal Communications (BICS), or social language, to promote peer relations and Cognitive Academic Language Proficiency (CALP) or academic language to make content comprehensible ▪ Engage and communicate effectively with linguistically and culturally diverse families and foster home-school connections	▪ Develop cultural competence and awareness by recognizing collectivistic vs. individualistic norms and expectations at home and school (e.g., nonverbal communication, haptics, gender norms, sleeping patterns) ▪ Avoid stereotyping and ethnic/racial microaggressions as well as neutrality when such comments are made in professional settings ▪ Distinguish among behavioral outbursts that result from lack of comprehension due to input that is inaccessible vs. those that are due to behavioral disorders ▪ Support immigrant families with the individualized education plans (IEPs) process and adopt a culturally affirming approach
Birch Elementary School	▪ Support the literacy and academic development of SLIFE ▪ Consider the socioemotional needs of SLIFE separated from family ▪ Differentiate instruction for limited English proficient SLIFE and integrate level-appropriate supports ▪ Consider effective push-in models that promote access and engagement for SLIFE in the mainstream classroom	▪ Assess educational backgrounds of SLIFE ▪ Integrate students with limited prior schooling experiences ▪ Distinguish between disability and language-based needs of SLIFE

Table I.1 (continued)
Chart of Cases and Pedagogies

Spawlding Public School	▪ Use strategies for supporting newcomers in the classroom ▪ Build background knowledge and oral language ▪ Support contextualized vocabulary instruction ▪ Acquire best practices for working with limited English proficient students in the mainstream classroom	▪ Support the learning needs of dual-diagnosed emerging bilingual learners who have physical disabilities (hearing impaired) and significant language disorders ▪ Provide scaffolds for promoting active engagement, comprehension, and vocabulary development for students with dual diagnoses
Inclusive Secondary		
College First High	▪ Scaffold learning for English learners with Universal Design for Learning (UDL) strategies to make content accessible ▪ Create a welcoming, safe, and nurturing context that lowers the affective filter ▪ Support learners' intrinsic and extrinsic motivation ▪ Promote listening comprehension and note-taking skills ▪ Support academic access and comprehension for English learners in a charter school, "no-excuses," rigorous academic context	▪ Incorporate trauma-informed strategies in the classroom for English learners ▪ Assess and support the socioemotional, acculturation, and educational needs of students who have experienced torture and trauma ▪ Understand the disproportionate discipline, retention, and achievement data between emerging bilinguals and their English-speaking peers ▪ Apply UDL approaches
South Bay Middle School	▪ Use WIDA language standards and Can Do Descriptors to develop level-appropriate curriculum ▪ Understand linguistic transfer and interlanguage in student writing ▪ Differentiate instruction to promote comprehension	▪ Assess newcomer students' socioemotional and acculturation needs and promote an inclusive teaching and learning context ▪ Liaise with community and families to support acculturation to the learning context and provide outreach and resources for families ▪ Structure newcomer and ELL success through inclusive curriculum and pedagogy ▪ Promote equitable educational opportunities for all

Table I.1 (continued)
Chart of Cases and Pedagogies

Forest Hills High School	▪ Scaffold reading and writing for elementary English learners in the mainstream classroom ▪ Differentiate instruction for emerging bilingual learners in the mainstream classroom	▪ Distinguish between learning disability and language acquisition ▪ Be aware of and support the needs of sociocultural backgrounds and needs of undocumented students ▪ Avoid the over-identification of English learners in Special Education by making informed assessments ▪ Know how to effectively use Response to Intervention and Progress Monitoring Systems
	Inclusive World Language	
Timberland High	▪ Make curricular and instructional connections for heritage language learners ▪ Promote oracy with inclusive practices ▪ Teach formal vs. informal language ▪ Use appropriate, balanced, and culturally responsive error correction	▪ Recognize and avoid microaggressions and linguistic racism and engage in inclusive practice for heritage learners ▪ Celebrate the diversity in the varieties of language and avoid linguistic discrimination ▪ Engage in culturally responsive teaching
Whittier Mountain High School	▪ Select and use authentic materials effectively ▪ Promote listening comprehension skills	▪ Make language learning accessible for students with ADHD and anxiety disorders
Adelesa High School	▪ Incorporate alternative formative and summative assessments in the foreign language classroom so students can demonstrate learning via multiple modalities (e.g., portfolios; project-based, real-world activities; demonstrations)	▪ Promote access to foreign language instruction for students with disabilities with differentiated teaching and assessment ▪ Embrace a strengths-based perspective of learners with disabilities in the world language classroom

Table I.1 (continued)
Chart of Cases and Pedagogies

<table>
<tr><th colspan="3">Inclusive Post-Secondary EAP</th></tr>
<tr><td>Northwood University</td><td>▪ Organize project-based and collaborative learning
▪ Thoughtfully group students</td><td>▪ Use inclusive teaching strategies for international students in core classes
▪ Pre-assess learners' profiles
▪ Avoid implicit bias
▪ Build inclusive learning environments via explicit ground rules</td></tr>
<tr><td>Fort Crimson Global Pathways</td><td>▪ Provide scaffolds for promoting academic writing in post-secondary settings for dual-diagnosed English learners in higher education</td><td>▪ Promote access to learning for visually impaired learners with UDL approaches
▪ Make course content accessible to dual-diagnosed learners in higher education
▪ Promote high expectations, inclusion, accessibility, and engagement for dual-diagnosed English learners in higher education</td></tr>
<tr><td>Shoreham English Language Institute</td><td>▪ Integrate strategies for promoting academic oral language development through equitable oral participation and sentence starters in EAP courses
▪ Use authentic texts to promote higher-order and critical thinking in EAP contexts
▪ Promote links between reading and speaking
▪ Include peer-to-peer feedback as a metacognitive support and inclusive assessment</td><td>▪ Incorporate inclusive teaching strategies such as establishing ground rules for respectful conversations in intercultural contexts
▪ Identify the needs of refugee students and other survivors of torture and trauma and tailored instructional and curricular decisions with cultural sensitivity
▪ Infuse culturally responsive teaching techniques such as multicultural texts and perspectives to promote cultural and linguistic competence
▪ Do not tolerate discrimination based on race, culture, or religion; navigate difficult conversations and be aware of implicit and explicit discrimination
▪ Embrace an openness to learning intersectional theories in the field of language learning that consider sociocultural aspects of language learning</td></tr>
</table>

References

Ellet, W. (2007). *The case study handbook.* Boston: Harvard Business School Press.

Gooden, A. B., & Zlateva, M. N. (2018). *A casebook for second language teacher education: Reflecting on the language classroom.* Ann Arbor: University of Michigan Press.

Waitoller, F., & Thorius, K. (2016). Cross-pollinating culturally sustaining pedagogy and universal design for learning. *Harvard Education Review, 86*(3), 366–389.

1

Case-Based Pedagogy and a Guide to Learning through Cases

Since the early 1990s, the field of second language teacher education (SLTE) has wrestled with the question of how best to prepare future educators and has gradually shifted to sociocultural approaches (Gooden & Zlateva, 2018). Vigorous professional debate has highlighted these issues in SLTE programs:

- a neglect for the sociocultural view of teaching and learning and an overemphasis on the teacher-centered, lecture-based model
- a need for critical reflection, rarely including the student teacher experiences into the curriculum
- a lack of a bridge between theory and practice
- poor modeling of critical-thinking strategies and learning processes (Freeman & Johnson, 2005; Hedgcock, 2002; Johnson, 2006; Richards, 2008; Smith, 2005; Tedick, 2005)

Two central aspects of L2 teacher preparation—knowledge base and pedagogy—have undergone scrutiny recently. The knowledge base has been re-examined to question the traditional language-based disciplines (linguistics and second language acquisition) as the core curriculum for SLTE (Freeman, 2002; Johnson & Golombek, 2011); there is now a call to incorporate learners' experiences and provide opportunities for reflective practice. Moreover, in a radical departure from the long-held rationalist view of teaching as transfer of knowledge, a sociocultural shift in traditional pedagogy urges SLTE education programs to create conditions for the co-construction of knowledge and understanding through social participation.

The current field of second language education is contextually diverse: It is concerned with the preparation of knowledgeable and skilled English as a second language, English as a foreign language, bilingual education, world language, and language immersion educators in national and international pre K–12 and post-secondary contexts. In the past, research in second language education was fragmented, and the field has only recently attempted to pull together all of its resources to gain a better understanding of SLTE and the issues facing the profession. In the process, case-based pedagogy, which utilizes both cases and the case method, has emerged as a particularly innovative instructional approach.

The core concepts of case-based pedagogy are reminiscent of Greek and Chinese philosophers of thought. It is a well-established pedagogy in schools of business, law, medicine, and social work. The research that does exist in teacher education programs employing the case method indicates that it successfully develops various types of teacher knowledge, teacher thinking, and self-efficacy (Moje & Wade, 1997; Shulman, 1992) and serves as modeling of good practice (Kaste, 2003). The results of two existing SLTE studies (Haley, 2008; Reichelt, 2000) that incorporated cases and case discussions point to the power of this method to address specific pedagogical needs in the field:

- understanding the practice of standards
- linking theoretical perspectives to practice
- differentiating instruction for diversity

The Case Method: Overview

The concepts of case and the case method are firmly defined in the fields of business, law, and medicine. Christensen and Hansen (1987) offer a clear definition from a business perspective:

> A case is a partial, historical, clinical study of a situation which has confronted a practicing administrator or managerial group. Presented in narrative form to encourage student involvement, it provides data—substantive and process—essential to an analysis of a specific situation, for the framing of alternative action programs, and for their implementation recognizing the complexity and ambiguity of the practical world. (p. 27)

The literature in teacher education, however, consists of multiple definitions, terminologies, and intended purposes. Essentially, it considers case a narrative representation of a real situation that places the reader(s) in the role of a participant in the situation. As Merseth (1996) notes:

> One common definition suggests that a case is a descriptive research document, often presented in narrative form that is based on a real-life situation or event. It attempts to convey a balanced, multidimensional representation of the context, participants, and reality of the situation. Cases are created explicitly for discussion and seek to include sufficient detail and information to elicit active analysis and interpretation by users with differing perspectives. (p. 722)

Case-based pedagogy is a means of developing teacher thinking, attitudes, and beliefs about issues in the field. Language teachers practicing it are not passive recipients of theories, principles, and strategies. Educators actively endeavor to accomplish goals they think to be important to their work (Clark & Peterson, 1986), and case studies give teachers the opportunity to reflect on their reasoning while providing an instrument that stimulates novel ways of thinking about decision-making and problem-solving.

Three key aspects of a case discussion are: (1) entering into a dialogical interaction with the self and others, (2) critical reflection, and (3) collaboration in a community of learning (Kleinfield, 1992). Users of this method first place themselves in the role of decision-maker as they read through the situation and identify the problem. The next step is to perform the necessary analysis—examining the causes and considering alternative courses of actions to determine a set of recommendations.

Specifically, the case studies with accompanying problem sets are designed to help practitioners develop language teacher knowledge, thinking, and praxis. The in-class discussions and problem sets encourage language educators who learn via this approach to make connections to their own practice.

During the case discussion process, participants learn how to analyze complex problems and perform the necessary research to confront authentic problems or test their proposed solutions. They probe the issues at stake and are compelled to exercise evidence-based judgment in the dynamic process of exchanging perspectives and opinions. Faced with constraints that would be present in the real world, they have to suggest a course of action, which trains them to assume responsibility. Participants are expected to read all the case materials in advance and consult with their peers in small groups before engaging with the entire class. They provide effective feedback on alternative courses so that, in the end, they have a set of recommendations.

Case Methodology

The case chapters open with a narrative that presents an authentic pedagogical dilemma in a specific educational context. In line with traditional case study structure, the narrative of the real-life situation is supplemented with what are referred to as **exhibits,** which provide additional information and evidentiary basis for the discussion of the case. The exhibits are various artifacts (e.g., policy documents, school demographic data and statistics, state and national teaching standards, and lesson plans and curricula) "curated" to reflect the sociocultural dimension of case studies, which heavily impacts current SLTE pedagogy. The framework for the case study consists of these stages:

1. Pre-case problem sets that ask participants to:
   a. **chart** the issues.
   b. **write** a discussion decision response paper.
2. In-class discussion through questions that cover these elements:
   a. **big-picture analysis** to describe the context of the case
   b. **stakeholders**, including a description of the key participants and their perspectives
   c. **surface issues** and problems that would be easy to identify in the case narratives at the pre-discussion stage
   d. **deep issues** that cover curricular and instructional challenges a language educator would discover after theoretically informed analysis
   e. **evidence-based solutions** that propose options for solving the cases with research-based strategies and pedagogical experience
   f. **teacher thinking prompts** that engage educators in critical and reflective practice
3. Post-case problem sets that ask the participants to:
   a. **categorize** their learning in terms of teacher knowledge, thinking, and dispositions.

b. **list** the learning objectives and implications for pedagogy as a way to move toward praxis.
c. **reflect on** connections between the case and previous and current teaching experience, as well as on key take-aways for future praxis, by developing an action plan and writing a short paper.
d. **discuss** the theoretical basis for behaviors and solutions and then continue to explore the issues presented by the case through suggested theoretical resources.
e. **consider** and **reflect** on other educators' perspectives and solutions through a set of authentic quotes that come from previous readers of the cases.

Each is followed by these problem sets:

I. Pre-Case Discussion Problem Sets

Complete the chart after reading the case.

Facts	
Opinions	
Assumptions	
Theories referred or connected to (if any)	
Ambiguous language	
Criteria you used in analyzing the case (e.g., emotional vs. rational)	
Emerging options	

Write a pre-case discussion decision paper. Include these points:

a. options for case resolution
b. criteria (a rational decision should always be made with a set of criteria)
c. analysis of options
d. recommendation (of the best choice among the options)
e. action plan

II. Case Discussion Questions

Under the skillful guidance of the case facilitator, students are expected to provide answers to a variety of questions. They consult with their peers in small groups before engaging with the entire class and do most of the talking as the case unfolds. It is imperative that the facilitator set an inclusive context and established ground rules for meaningful and respectful conversations. A pre-case, whole group discussion that addresses these questions is an important suggested activity to set the stage for inclusive case study discussions:

- How can we ensure that everyone feels comfortable, confident, valued, and heard during these case study discussions?
- What is the value of sharing diverse opinions, values, and lived experiences?
- How can we make room for diverse perspectives and respectfully disagree?
- What are strategies for demonstrating active and empathentic listening?
- What are expectations for demonstrating tolerance and respect?
- What behaviors and comments should be avoided?

Big-Picture Analysis

Describe the context of the case.

Stakeholders

In small groups, assume the role of one of the case stakeholders. Write a statement/dialogue expressing this person's or group's hypothetical feelings and perspectives. Be prepared to act out your roles to the large group.

Surface Issues

What are the surface issues in this case? What is happening here from an untrained perspective? What underlying assumptions or beliefs feed into this perspective?

Deep Issues

Discuss the real issues in the case. Try to categorize them in terms of language teaching curriculum and instruction.

Evidence-Based Solutions

In groups, develop evidence-based solutions for each deep issue listed. Whenever possible, refer to a theory or principle of language learning and teaching to support your proposed solutions.

Teacher Thinking

In what ways does this case influence and/or reinforce your beliefs and dispositions as a teacher? Consult the Further Reading and Resources to help with theoretically informed solutions.

III. Post-Case Problem Sets

Post-Case Analysis

A. Categorize what you learned as:
   - teacher knowledge and praxis (e.g., content knowledge, curricular knowledge, pedagogical content knowledge and application)
   - teacher thinking (e.g., beliefs, problem-solving strategies, prioritizing objectives, values, professional ethics, attitudes)

B. List:
   - learning objectives that you discovered in the case
   - potential learning outcomes
   - implications for your pedagogical practices

C. The post-case problem sets introduce reactions from various perspectives. These quotes are from others who have read the cases for educational and pedagogical purposes. Read all of the quotes and then choose two about which you write a short response (put the quotes at the top of each response). Use these questions as a guide:
   - What is the message the speaker is trying to convey? If possible, also explain why you chose the quote.
   - What examples can you think of that connect to the themes presented?
   - Can you relate the quote to a class discussion or to something you have read or experienced?

<u>Note</u>: The quotes are composites based on observations by both experienced and inexperienced teachers and are included to illustrate genuine (therefore occasionally extreme) reactions of practitioners to classroom situations similar to the scenarios in the cases. Some quotes may reveal an insufficient knowledge base, while others serve to illuminate good teacher instincts. Some quotes are purposefully provocative in order to trigger debate and reveal unspoken prejudices and stereotypes (sometimes witnessed in teacher rooms or watercooler talk). My experience shows that the value of such statements lies in helping teachers (1) to develop the ability to reflect on holistic aspects of their teaching and (2) to categorize their experiences in terms of teacher knowledge, thinking, and praxis.

D. Write a reflection describing a take-away from the case in terms of praxis. Make sure to develop an action plan to resolve the case. Consider these questions as guidelines:
   - In what ways did the case discussion influence your thinking about the case?
   - Did you change your original decision or did the discussion reaffirm your position?
   - What points had you not considered prior to the case discussion?
   - How might the information you gained from this case be applicable to your current instructional setting and/or future instructional settings?
   - What did you learn?
   - What are you inspired to learn more about?
   - How did the themes discussed in class apply to your experience?

E. Discuss what theoretical basis there is for:
   - the stakeholders' behavior in the case.
   - the solutions you proposed.

Further Reading and Resources

The further readings are intended to provide the theoretical underpinnings for the discussions and can be used either in preparation for the case (for students with less methodological training) or as an extension of learning after the discussion (for participants with solid formative training). They inform case solutions based on research and best practices.

References and Additional Resources

Christensen, C.R., & Hansen, A.J. (1987). *Teaching and the case method.* Boston: Harvard Business School.

Clark, C. M., & Peterson, P. L. (1986). Teachers' thought processes. In M. C. Witrock (Ed.), *Handbook of research on teaching* (3rd ed., pp. 255–296). New York: Macmillan.

Ellet, W. (2007). *The case study handbook.* Boston: Harvard Business School Press.

Freeman, D. (2002). The hidden side of the work: Teacher knowledge and learning to teach. *Language Teaching, 35,* 1–3.

Freeman, D., & Johnson, K. E. (1998). Reconceptualizing the knowledge-base of language teacher education. *TESOL Quarterly, 32*(3), 397–417.

Freeman, D., & Johnson, K. E. (2005). Toward linking teacher knowledge and student learning. In D. J. Tedick (Ed.), *Second language teacher education: International perspectives* (pp. 73–95). Mahwah, NJ: Lawrence Erlbaum.

Gooden, A., & Zlateva, A. (2018). *A casebook for second language teacher education: Reflecting on the language classroom.* Ann Arbor: University of Michigan Press.

Haley, M. (2008). Implications of using case study instruction in a second/foreign language classroom. *Foreign Language Annals, 37*(2), 290–300.

Hedgcock, J. S. (2002). Toward a socioliterate approach to second language teacher education. *Modern Language Journal, 86*(3), 299–317.

Johnson, K. E. (2006). The sociocultural turn and its challenges for second language teacher education. *TESOL Quarterly, 40*(1), 235–257.

Johnson, K. E. (2009). *Second language teacher education: A sociocultural perspective.* New York: Routledge.

Johnson, K. E., & Golombek, P. R. (Eds.). (2011). *Research on second language teacher education: A sociocultural perspective on professional development.* New York: Routledge.

Kaste, J. (2003). Scaffolding through cases: Diverse constructivist teaching in the literacy methods course. *Teacher and Teacher Education, 20,* 31–45.

Kleinfeld, J. (1992). Learning to think like a teacher: The study of cases. In J. H. Shulman (Ed.), *Case methods in teacher education* (pp. 33–49). New York: Teachers College Press.

Merseth, K. (1996). Cases and case methods in teacher education. In J. Sikula (Ed.), *Handbook of research on teacher education* (pp. 102–119). New York: Macmillan.

Moje, E. B., & Wade, S. E. (1997). What case discussions reveal about teacher thinking. *Teaching and Teacher Education, 13,* 691–712.

Reichelt, M. (2000). Case studies in L2 teacher education. *ELT Journal, 54*(4), 346–353.

Richards, J. (2008). Second language teacher education today. *RELC Journal, 39*(2), 158–176.

Shulman, L. S. (1986). Those who understand: Knowledge growth in teaching. *Educational Researcher, 15*(2), 4–14.

Shulman, L. S. (1992). Toward a pedagogy of cases. In J. Shulman (Ed.), *Case methods in teacher education* (pp. 1–30). New York: Teachers College Press.

Smith, L. (2005). The impact of action research on teacher collaboration and professional growth. In D. J. Tedick (Ed.), *Second language teacher education: International perspectives* (pp. 199–204). Mahwah, NJ: Lawrence Erlbaum.

Tarone, E., & Allwright, D. (2005). Language teacher-learning and student language-learning: Shaping the knowledge base. In D. J. Tedick (Ed.), *Second language teacher education: International perspectives* (pp. 5–23). Mahwah, NJ: Lawrence Erlbaum.

Tedick, D. J. (2005). *Second language teacher education: International perspectives.* Mahwah, NJ: Lawrence Erlbaum.

Wright, T. (2010). Second language teacher education: Review of recent research on practice. *Language Teaching, 43*(3), 259–296.

2

Cases in Elementary Settings: Inclusive ESL/SEI/Bilingual Education

The cases in this chapter raise a range of contemporary issues concerning the education of elementary English earners in a variety of educational contexts. The first case, *Mountain Ridge Elementary School,* takes place in a special education referral meeting, in which teachers express concerns about an emerging bilingual learner whose family immigrated from Cape Verde and who needed a referral for a behavioral disorder. This case focuses on the need for teachers to acquire cultural competence and sensitivity when working with culturally and linguistically diverse learners and their families and to integrate social and academic language in their lessons to support the acculturation of immigrant learners. The second case, *Birch Elementary School,* places the reader in the position of teachers who need to support the literacy development and academic success of a SLIFE with limited prior schooling experiences and who struggle to distinguish between learning disabilities and language barriers. The third case, *Spawlding Public School,* presents the reader with the opportunities and challenges of supporting the learning needs of emerging dual-diagnosed bilingual learners with physical disabilities (hearing impaired) and significant spoken and language disorders.

This chapter is designed to offer an open-ended forum for discussing important educational issues such as:

- teaching BICS and CALP, or social and academic English
- fostering home-school connections and engaging positively with diverse families
- scaffolding language and learning supports for students with limited to no prior schooling
- distinguishing between learning disability and language difference
- differentiating literacy instruction to support students with varying needs
- distinguishing among behavioral outbursts that result from lack of comprehension due to input that is inaccessible versus those that are due to behavioral disorders
- promoting access for dually diagnosed students, or English learners with physical or cognitive disabilities
- incorporating culturally responsive pedagogy and holistic assessment

CASE 2.1

Mountain Ridge Elementary School

Mountain Ridge Elementary School serves a multicultural, multilingual community and prides itself on celebrating and welcoming its diverse families (see Exhibit A). The population of Mountain Ridge is 64 percent Hispanic or Latinx, 3 percent Cape Verdean and Portuguese/Brazilian, 17 percent white, and 11 percent Black or African American. The school's mission is to prepare students with 21st century skills such as creativity, collaboration, critical thinking, communication, and a growth mindset. Although the principal has expressed a concern about hiring more culturally and linguistically diverse educators, the majority of teachers in the district are white and monolingual. During the last annual anti-bias workshop, quite a few teachers admitted that they find it very challenging to communicate effectively with diverse families and to establish home school connections.

The six educators in the room during a special education referral included Chrissy, the kindergarten teacher; Janet, the social worker; Robyn, the English Language Learner (ELL) coordinator; the special education teachers; and Peter, the school principal. Maritza, the Spanish translator, was also present in the room. Chrissy had prompted this meeting because of her concerns about Joao's behavior (Joao had been held back in kindergarten).

"His father is late. He is always late. Who knows if he will even show up," exclaimed Chrissy, who just completed her Master's in Elementary Education from the state college.

"Let's give it five more minutes. I will give him a call. He always picks up my calls," said the school principal.

Chrissy replied, "Good for you. I can never get him to respond to **any** of my emails."

The atmosphere in the room was uncomfortably hostile as everyone dove into their smartphones or typed vigorously as they responded to emails while waiting. Joao's father, Manuel, came 20 minutes late. He did not speak English, so a translator was made available to help him to understand the purpose of the meeting regarding his son. The only issue was that Manuel spoke Cape Verdean Creole, and the translator spoke Spanish. The principal apologized but said, "I am sure you will figure it out. Aren't the languages similar?" Manuel smiled and nodded his head. Fortunately, Robyn (the ELL Coordinator) present was fluent in Portuguese, so she helped fill in some of the linguistic gaps. Although Cape Verdean Creole is the home language of the majority of the population, the language of schooling is Portuguese, so Manuel was luckily able to decode at least the gist of the meeting.

The meeting promptly began with, unfortunately, no introduction or mention of Joao's strengths. In fact, the group got right down to business with no small talk or any welcoming of the father upon his entry. The meeting started with a summary of the behaviors that were causing concern. Specifically, the teachers felt that Joao should be referred for behavioral concerns since, *from their perspective*, he was overly hands-on and verbally aggressive with peers his age. Although the teachers had attended the one mandatory anti-bias educator training, none of them brought to the meeting lived intercultural experiences. They serve a very ethnically and racially diverse school, but most of the teachers in the school come from white, historically privileged, and monolingual backgrounds.

In an effort to explore Joao's behavior, the kindergarten teacher began to ask Manuel about the extent to which inappropriate behavior is exhibited or even supported at home.

Chrissy began by stating:

> I want us to be mindful that there is a lot of inappropriate behavior and some of it can be age appropriate and typical and some of it can be learned behavior somewhere else so I want to just be able to explore with Joao's dad a little bit. We didn't know last year, and his dad told you, that they wrestle around at home and play around in their underwear, things like that, so I guess I am just looking for…does he see this at home? What are the boundaries at home? Are people allowed to be in the bathroom together or do they shower with the doors open? Do kids play around like this at home? Is aggressive verbal language tolerated at home? I think we need to get to the root of this learned behavior.

The father was clearly uncomfortable with this type of questioning after gathering the gist of the poorly translated summaries and stated, "No, we are just a normal, loving family."

Robyn jumped into the dialogue with some hesitation. She said, "Can we start with a strengths-based perspective about Joao and his family? I mean, would you like to share anything positive that you have observed with Joao this year?"

Ignoring the father's response and dismissing Robyn's suggestion, Chrissy said, "Yeah, I would say, overall, academically, it is helping him to be in kindergarten again. He is just more ready for all of the learning. But again, you want to continue to push him to meet all his goals. In math, he is doing much better. He is one of our higher math scholars. He can count up to 130; he can identify and write his numbers; he can count by 10. He doesn't know all of his shapes yet, but he is on his way."

However, Chrissy then continued with negative remarks: "Also, Joao has a lot of difficulties keeping his body calm and still. We have tried a lot of different things in the classroom to help him, so he that can help keep his hands busy while he is trying to learn."

As she talked, Maritza and Robyn scrambled to find ways to help Manuel understand the translation of Chrissy's remarks.

Chrissy continued, "So he displays a lot of difficulty doing any kinds of sitting or sitting for a long time. We will give him a look so we don't always put him in 'time out,' and sometimes he responds to the look and returns to his seat. But it's just that he is disrupting the entire class, which tends to be half of the time."

A special education teacher chimed in, "Would you say that he is more active than kids his age?" "Yes," Chrissy replied. Then the social worker asked, "Are you seeing that at home?" The father replied, "No. He might behave a little bit like that around his mother but never when I am around."

Chrissy added, "Also, the other piece that we are concerned with is his socioemotional ability to have conversations with his friends that are appropriate. Sometimes the language that he uses is not always appropriate. Sometimes with his body, he does things that are not appropriate."

"Can you give us some examples so we can help dad with specific examples?" asked Robyn.

Chrissy answered, "With words he commands his friends around. He touches his friends too much and hugs people without their consent."

Robyn responded, "Just from the language learning perspective: sometimes behavior outbursts could be the result of a lack of general comprehension, so that is something we need to factor in. It is common, and just where he is at in terms of language development. His social language vocabulary is probably limited and influenced by interlanguage, making him sound strange or inappropriate at times. In addition, we need to think of ways to build his cognitive academic language proficiency so that he can meet grade-level expectations. A lot of this could be language based or even culture based."

Chrissy laughed and then added, "Sure, I think language may have something to do with it, but I definitely I know there is something much more than language going on."

The special education teacher chimed in, "Yes, I mean we have been seeing inappropriate language and touching since last year."

After considering Robyn's remarks, Chrissy stated, "Well, it could be that that is his way of using language and his body to make friends. I don't know that he necessarily knows appropriate kindergarten play."

The social worker then added, "I think there is something more than language. We have been seeing concerns with inappropriate touching and language since last year. That's his way of trying to make friends or trying to be socially appropriate. I don't know if he knows appropriate play."

Peter added, "I think language is a big piece of it. I think he struggles with how to have appropriate conversations, and I know that in English he doesn't always use full sentences unless he is prompted with 'Try it again, or say it like this.'"

As the meeting concluded, everyone agreed that Joao should be observed by the ELL coordinator. Given the fact that Joao scored an overall score of 2.2 on the WIDA language test and due to his cultural differences, Robyn believes that language and cultural differences could be the causes of his classroom behavioral challenges. To help Chrissy understand what is meant by culturally responsive pedagogy and in response to what she perceived to be a poorly managed meeting with a parent from another culture and who speaks another language, Robyn emailed her and all who were present a memo (see Exhibit B) with a chart of differences between individualistic cultures like the U.S. and collectivistic cultures like Cape Verde. She also wrote an email with a list of Can Do activities for Level 2 students for teachers to consider integrating (see Exhibit C).

Exhibit A: Mountain Ridge Elementary School Diversity Statement

Mountain Ridge Elementary School seeks to reflect the increasingly diverse world in which our students presently live and will live in the future. We intend to provide our students with a superior education in a community of students, parents, faculty, and staff that represents a variety of racial, ethnic, cultural, and religious backgrounds. We strive to ensure respect for all regardless of sex, gender, gender identity, race, religion, sexual orientation, ability, family structure, or economic background.

Exhibit B: Memo to Teacher with Chart of Differences between Individual and Collective Cultures

<table>
<tr>
<td>1. The pivotal unit is the I or individual.
2. Space and privacy are important.
3. Communication tends to be direct, explicit, and personal.
4. Educational context is transactional and competitive.</td>
<td>1. The pivotal unit is the we or the group.
2. Space and privacy are less important than relationships.
3. Communication is intuitive, complex, and impressionistic.
4. Educational context is relational and collaborative.</td>
</tr>
</table>

Exhibit C: Can Do Activities for Level 2 from ELL Coordinator

Dear Chrissy,

Based on the fact that Joao's English language proficiency level was 2, he is considered limited English proficient and you can expect him to engage in the following speaking tasks, which come from the WIDA website (www.wida.wisc.edu).

LEVEL 2 Learners CAN DO:

Recount by:
• re-stating some language associated with illustrated short stories or informational text *(e.g., "I see"* or *"I hear").*

• re-enacting various roles when interacting in pairs or in small groups.

Explain by:
• describing uses of everyday objects or roles of familiar people *(e.g., "Teacher reads").*

• stating attributes and classifying objects into illustrated categories to show how they go together *(e.g., shapes, colors, sizes).*

Do not hesitate to reach out to me for examples of how to support Joao's academic success and linguistic development.

Cordially,

Robyn

I. Pre-Case Discussion Problem Sets

Complete the chart after reading the case.

Facts	
Opinions	
Assumptions	
Theories referred or connected to (if any)	
Ambiguous language	
Criteria you used in analyzing the case (e.g., emotional vs. rational)	
Emerging options	

Write a pre-case discussion decision paper. Include these points:

a. options for case resolution
b. criteria (a rational decision should always be made with a set of criteria)
c. analysis of options
d. recommendation (of the best choice among the options)
e. action plan

II. Case Discussion Questions

Big-Picture Analysis

Describe the context of the case.

- student and educator demographics
- school mission
- education plan referral meeting structure

Stakeholders

In small groups, assume the role of one of the case stakeholders. Write a statement/ dialogue expressing this person's or group's hypothetical feelings and perspectives. Be prepared to act out your roles to the large group.

- Chrissy
- Joao
- Manuel
- Robyn
- Janet
- Special education teachers
- Social service teacher
- Maritza

Surface Issues

What are the surface issues in this case? What is happening here from an untrained perspective? What underlying assumptions or beliefs feed into this perspective?

Deep Issues

Discuss the real issues in the case. Try to categorize them in terms of language teaching curriculum and instruction.

Evidence-Based Solutions

In groups, develop evidence-based solutions for each deep issue listed. Whenever possible, refer to a theory or principle of language learning and teaching to support your proposed solutions.

Teacher Thinking

In what ways does this case influence and/or reinforce your beliefs and dispositions as a teacher? Consult the Further Reading and Resources section to help with theoretically informed solutions.

III. Post-Case Problem Sets

Post-Case Analysis

A. Categorize what you learned as:
   - teacher knowledge and praxis (e.g., content knowledge, curricular knowledge, pedagogical content knowledge and application)
   - teacher thinking (e.g., beliefs, problem-solving strategies, prioritizing objectives, values, professional ethics, attitudes)

B. List:
   - learning objectives that you discovered in the case
   - potential learning outcomes
   - implications for pedagogical practices

C. The post-case problem sets introduce reactions from various perspectives. These quotes are from others who have read the cases for educational and pedagogical purposes. Read all of the quotes and then choose two quotes about which to write a short response (put the quotes at the top of each response). Use these questions as a guide:
   - What is the message the speaker is trying to convey? If possible, also explain why you chose the quote.
   - What examples can you think of that connect to the themes presented?
   - Can you relate the quote to a class discussion or to something you have read or experienced?

Quotes

1. "It would be valuable for the teacher to gather information about Joao's background to determine what might be causing his outbursts. It is customary to get a social history of learners we are concerned about."
2. "Perhaps Chrissy should incorporate more activities that help to promote Joao's social English to support his peer relations. The teacher should incorporate more on-task or hands-on activities that will help to make content accessible to him as an emerging bilingual learner. Also, the teacher can incorporate more peer-to-peer interaction so that the students have more of a purpose for discussion rather than disrupting the class."
3. "Many of the parents have to work during the day—some at jobs with extremely long hours. It is difficult for them to come to school during the day to participate in meetings such as individual education plan meetings. The teacher should try providing alternative times for parents to get involved at the school by perhaps hosting some activities after or before school."
4. "We should be careful about judging families who come from different cultural orientations. Even though certain behaviors or speech patterns may seem strange or inappropriate, they could be influenced by the learners' native languages and cultures and we should identify and support their acculturation."

D. Write a reflection describing a take-away from the case in terms of praxis. Make sure to develop an action plan to resolve the case. Consider these questions as guidelines:

- In what ways did the case discussion influence your thinking about the case?
- Did you change your original decision or did the discussion reaffirm your position?
- What points had you not considered prior to the case discussion?
- How might the information you gained from this case be applicable to your current instructional setting and/or future instructional settings?
- What did you learn?
- What are you inspired to learn more about?
- How did the themes discussed in class apply to your experience?

E. Discuss what theoretical basis there is for:
   - the stakeholders' behaviors in the case.
   - the solutions you proposed.

Further Reading and Resources

Brown, S., & Eisterhold, J. (2004). *Topics in language and culture for teachers.* Ann Arbor: University of Michigan Press.

DeCapua, A. (2018). *Culture myths: Applying second language research to classroom teaching.* Ann Arbor: University of Michigan Press.

Collier, C. (2014). *What every administrator should know about separating differences and disabilities: A webinar for school administrators.* Retrieved from http://www.doe.in.gov/sites/default/files/elme/schadmins-2014.pdf

Cummins, J. (2000a). BICS and CALP. In M. Byram (Ed.), *Routledge encyclopedia of language teaching and learning* (pp. 76–79). New York: Routledge.

Cummins, J. (2000b). *Language, power and pedagogy: Bilingual children in the crossfire.* Clevedon, England: Multilingual Matters.

Cummins, J. (2008). BICS and CALP: Empirical and theoretical status of the distinction. In B. Street & N. H. Hornberger (Eds.), *Encyclopedia of language and education* (pp. 71–83). New York: Springer Science.

De Gaetano, Y. (2007). The role of culture in engaging Latino parents' involvement in school. *Urban Education, 42,* 145–162.

Echevaria, J., Vogt, M., & Short, D. (2013). *Making content comprehensible for English learners: The SIOP model.* Upper Saddle River, NJ: Pearson Education.

Gottlieb, M. (2006). *Assessing English language learners: Bridges from language proficiency to academic achievement.* Thousand Oaks, CA: Corwin Press.

Haynes, J., & Zacarian, D. (2010). *Teaching English language learners across the content areas.* Alexandria, VA: ASCD.

Hofstede, G. (2001). *Cultures consequences: Comparing values, behaviors, institutions and organizations across nations* (2nd ed.). London: Sage.

Klingner, J. K., & Harry, B. (2006). The special education referral and decision-making process for English language learners: Child study team meetings and placement conferences. *Teacher College Record, 108*(11), 2247–2281.

Kubota, R., & Lin, A. (2009). *Race, class, identity in second language education: Exploring critically engaged practice.* New York: Routledge.

Lippi-Green, R. (2012). *English with an accent: Language ideology and discrimination in the United States* (2nd ed.). New York: Routledge.

Mihai, F. (2017). *Assessing English learners in the content areas: A research-into-practice guide for educators* (2nd ed.). Ann Arbor: University of Michigan Press.

Paradis, J., Genesee, F., & Crago, M. B. (2010). *Dual language development and disorders: A handbook on bilingualism and second language learning* (2nd ed.). Baltimore: Brookes.

Ramirez, A.Y. (2008). Immigrant families and schools: The need for a better relationship. In T. Turner-Vorbeck & M. M. March (Eds.), *Other kinds of families: Diversity in schools and culture* (pp. 28–45). New York: Teachers College Press.

Santos, R.M., & Ostrosky, M. M. (2015). *Understanding the impact of language differences on classroom behavior* (What Works Brief No. 2 Series). Nashville: Center on the Social and Emotional Foundations for Early Learning. Retrieved from http://csefel.vanderbilt.edu/briefs/wwb2.pdf

Sauer, J., & Rosetti, Z. (2019). *Affirming disability: Strengths-based portraits of culturally diverse families.* New York: Teachers College Press.

Shim, J. (2017). Self-identified linguistic microaggressions among monolingual pre-service teachers: Why they matter for English language learners. *Multicultural Learning and Teaching, 12*(2), doi.org/10.1515/mlt-2016-0017

Tabors, P. O. (1997). *One child, two languages: A guide for preschool educators of children learning English as a second language.* Newton, MA: Butterworth-Heinemann.

Zhang, C., & Bennett, T. (2003) Facilitating the meaningful participation of culturally and linguistically diverse families in the IFSP and IEP process. *Focus on Autism and Other Developmental Disabilities, 18*(1), 51–59.

CASE 2.2

Birch Elementary School

The school's special education director called Johanny's stepmother to express her concerns. She disclosed that Johanny moved to the United States from the Dominican Republic when she was in the third grade. Johanny did not have any exposure to English before the third grade. While in the Dominican Republic, Johanny did not attend school nor did she have experiences with print literacy in her native Spanish language. She is the first SLIFE that the Birch Elementary School has received, and no one seems to know how to best support her learning. The school district, which was once predominately white working class, has seen a significant increase in the number of immigrant students in the past five years, so the principal decided recently that it would be a good idea to hire an ELL Coordinator to support teachers in their knowledge growth of strategies for supporting bilingual students. The stepmother reported that Johanny lived with her mother and other siblings in a rural part of the country where daily survival and staving off hunger were bigger priorities than attending school that was more than 20 miles away by foot.

Johanny attended the third and fourth grades in another town before attending fifth grade at Birch Elementary School. When Johanny was in the fourth grade, her parents referred her to the special education evaluation team. At that time, Johanny was not found eligible because of her limited English proficiency and lack of adequate instruction. Her WIDA scores indicate that she is a Level 2 English learner overall. The bilingual speech pathologist tested Johanny's expressive and receptive skills in her native language, and the results indicate that she has limited expressive and receptive skills in her native Spanish. Ms. Riveira and Ms. Tucker, Johanny's math and English Language Arts (ELA) teachers, made a referral to the special education evaluation team because of Johanny's academic performance in both math and ELA classes, which included difficulty retaining procedural knowledge for mathematics, difficulty with basic computation skills including addition and subtraction with regrouping, and limited understanding of the base-ten number system. Johanny then worked with the special education teacher, Shirley, because before the newly hired ELL Coordinator's arrival, the mainstream teachers did not know how to help her.

Shirley summarizes her unofficial special education support for Johanny outlined in a memo:

- She is learning 40–50 words per week using Lakeshore® cards (e.g., school supplies, food, and clothes).
- She has trouble on STEP® literacy test showing what she knows because the test is all verbal (e.g., Where is the first place the girl looks? She does not know where "first" is. Need to teach the words *first* and *last*).
- Scaffold reading with flashcards and visuals; she circles cards she finds; teacher writes sentence and teacher has her read out loud and then circle sight words; sometimes takes away visual for scaffolds.
- She sees me four days a week for an hour and half.
- She is working on matching and sorting (things we wear, things we eat).
- She is practicing sentence starters as well as working to complete sentences.
- She is doing multi-digit arithmetic. She does not have a concept of 10s and 1s. We have done 10s rods and digi-blocks, but it is an abstract concept. Difficult for her to master but important to teach.
- She is struggling to learn even and odd numbers.
- I suggested that she use games or manipulatives.
- I don't know how to support her with tests.

Despite six months of math interventions, Johanny continued to earn 1s and 2s on her math exit tickets. (Exit tickets are informal assessments.) Her retention, even during small-group work, is low. However, a closer look at the small-group makeup reveals that Johanny had no peer models or bilingual peers to help support learning. In ELA, Johanny continued to struggle with reading comprehension and fluency. She was in the whole class with additional push-in support from teachers and peer models. Despite these interventions, she continued to fail all formal and informal classroom-based assessments.

According to the state educational policy and regulatory board on special education, there are clear guidelines on the pre-referral process: "Sometimes, challenges can be addressed in the mainstream classroom using interventions available within the general education program. The school district must record a history of attempted classroom interventions before referring a child for special education evaluation." Exhibit A details the classroom interventions that have been tried to ameliorate the presenting problem prompting referral. Exhibit B shows test scores.

The ELL Coordinator developed a support plan (see Exhibit C) for Johanny and shared it with the teachers. However, every time the ELL Coordinator entered the classroom to observe the teachers, she almost never saw any of the language-based strategies implemented by the teachers, aside from think-pair-share and peer supports. The ELL Coordinator felt that it was still hard to rule out language if these language supports had not been instituted faithfully in the classroom: "It is against my best nature to refer this student to special education if she is still not receiving adequate English language support and scaffolding." Even when the ELL Coordinator observed the small-group math and ELA interventions, she saw that Johanny often struggled to understand because the teachers were explaining or asking questions far beyond Johanny's current level of comprehensibility.

Exhibit A: History of Classroom Interventions for Johanny

Start Intervention	Intervention
9/5	Small-group math instruction, a few days per week
9/7	Small-group ELA instruction one or more days a week; frequent reminders to stay focused
11/6	Small-group instruction during math class five days per week for 110 minutes
11/6	Frequent check-ins; circle back often to previously learned concepts in math
11/12	Small group every day for 80–100 minutes for ELA
12/11	Return to whole-group instruction in math with additional push-in teacher in the classroom; partner with peer models for academic conversations

Exhibit B: ACCESS® Overall and Literacy Scores

3rd Grade Overall	4th Grade Overall
2.0	3.7

3rd Grade Literacy	4th Grade Literacy
1.9	2.5

Exhibit C: Support Recommendations from the ELL Coordinator

Focus Areas	Support Recommendations
1. Speaking	• Think-pair-share • Structured debates • Require use of academic language with sentence frames • Reciprocal teaching • Include oral presentations
2. Reading	• Word banks • Extra wait time • Graphic organizers • Think-pair-share • Require full sentence responses • Guided reading and small groups • Audio books • Resources for transition words • Teacher read-aloud • Visual glossaries • 1:1 DBQ support in classroom
3. Writing	• Graphic organizers to assist with writing structure • Small-group support • Writing conferences to target specific areas of need • Mentor texts

I. Pre-Case Discussion Problem Sets

Complete the chart after reading the case.

Facts	
Opinions	
Assumptions	
Theories referred or connected to (if any)	
Ambiguous language	
Criteria you used in analyzing the case (e.g., emotional vs. rational)	
Emerging options	

Write a pre-case discussion decision paper. Include these points:

a. options for case resolution
b. criteria (a rational decision should always be made with a set of criteria)
c. analysis of options
d. recommendation (of the best choice among the options)
e. action plan

II. Case Discussion Questions

Big-Picture Analysis

Describe the context of the case.

- prior learning context and current learning context
- push-in model

Stakeholders

In small groups, assume the role of one of the case stakeholders. Write a statement/ dialogue expressing this person's or group's hypothetical feelings and perspectives. Be prepared to act out your roles to the large group.

- Johanny
- Ms. Riviera
- Ms. Tucker
- Johanny's stepmother
- Shirley
- ELL Coordinator

Surface Issues

What are the surface issues in this case? What is happening here from an untrained perspective? What underlying assumptions or beliefs feed into this perspective?

Deep Issues

Discuss the real issues in the case. Try to categorize them in terms of language teaching curriculum and instruction.

Evidence-Based Solutions

In groups, develop evidence-based solutions for each deep issue listed. Whenever possible, refer to a theory or principle of language learning and teaching to support your proposed solutions.

Teacher Thinking

In what ways does this case influence and/or reinforce your beliefs and dispositions as a teacher? Consult the Further Readings and Resources section to help with theoretically informed solutions.

III. Post-Case Problem Sets

Post-Case Analysis

A. Categorize what you learned as:
   - teacher knowledge and praxis (e.g., content knowledge, curricular knowledge, pedagogical content knowledge and application)
   - teacher thinking (e.g., beliefs, problem-solving strategies, prioritizing objectives, values, professional ethics, attitudes)

B. List:
   - learning objectives that you discovered in the case
   - potential learning outcomes
   - implications for your pedagogical practices

C. The post-case problem sets introduce reactions from various perspectives. These quotes are from others who have read the cases for educational and pedagogical purposes. Read all of the quotes and then choose two about which to write a short response (put the quotes at the top of each response). Use the questions as a guide:
   - What is the message the speaker(s) is trying to convey? If possible, also explain why you chose the quote.
   - What examples can you think of that connect to the themes presented?
   - Can you relate the quote to a class discussion or to something you have read or experienced?

Quotes

1. "This student needs to be in a self-contained classroom. It is too much work for a teacher to support a learner with such huge gaps in the mainstream classroom even with push-in supports."
2. "This is an example of how and why collaboration is key. To truly support Johanny, it is the responsibility of the teachers—both push-in and mainstream—to communicate about effective push-in models. Also, collaboration with the special education team is important as well as the family."
3. "We have to be really careful about referring English learners to special education referrals without adequate documentation that language barriers have been addressed. Too many teachers want to jump to the special education conclusion."

D. Write a reflection describing a take-away from the case in terms of praxis. Make sure to develop an action plan to resolve the case. Consider these questions as guidelines:

- In what ways did the case discussion influence your thinking about the case?
- Did you change your original decision or did the discussion reaffirm your position?
- What points had you not considered prior to the case discussion?
- How might the information you gained from this case be applicable to your current instructional setting and/or future instructional settings?
- What did you learn?
- What are you inspired to learn more about?
- How did the themes discussed in class apply to your experience?

E. Discuss what theoretical basis there is for:

- the stakeholders' behavior in the case.
- the solutions you proposed.

Further Reading and Resources

DeCapua, A. (2019). *SLIFE: What every teacher needs to know.* Ann Arbor: University of Michigan Press.

DeCapua, A., & Marshall, H. (2011). Reaching ELLs at risk: Instruction for students with limited or interrupted formal education. *Preventing School Failure, 55*(1), 35–41.

DeCapua, A., Marshall, H., & Tang, L. (2020). *Meeting the needs of SLIFE* (2nd ed.). Ann Arbor: University of Michigan Press.

Echevarria, J., Vogt M. E., & Short, D. (2012). *Making content comprehensible for English learners: The SIOP model* (4th ed.). Boston: Pearson.

Fillmore, L. W., & Snow, C. (2000). *What teachers need to know about language.* ERIC database ED444379. Washington, DC: Center for Applied Linguistics.

Freeman, Y., & Freeman, D. (2002). *Closing the achievement gap: How to reach limited-formal-schooling and long-term English learners.* Portsmouth, NH: Heinemann.

Hamayan, E., Marler, B., Sanchez-Lopez, C., & Damico, J. (2013). *Special education considerations for English language learners: Delivering a continuum of services.* Philadelphia: Caslon.

Robertson, K., & Lafond, S. How to support ELL students with interrupted formal education (SIFEs). Retrieved from www.colorincolorado.org.

Snow, M., & Brinton, D. (2020). *Content-based language instruction: What every ESL teacher needs to know.* Ann Arbor: University of Michigan Press.

WIDA. (2012). 2012 amplification of the English language development standards: Kindergarten–grade 12. Madison: Board of Regents at the University of Wisconsin System. Retrieved from https://wida.wisc.edu/resources/2012-amplification-wida-english-language-development-standards

WIDA. (2012). Can do descriptors. Madison: Board of Regents at the University of Wisconsin System.

WIDA. (2015). WIDA focus on SLIFE: Students with limited or interrupted formal education (WIDA Focus Bulletins). Madison: Wisconsin Center for Education Research. Retrieved from https://wida.wisc.edu/resources/students-limited-or-interrupted-formal-education-slife

Zacrian, D., & Haynes, J. (2012). *The essential guide for educating beginning English learners.* Thousand Oaks, CA: Corwin Press.

CASE 2.3

Spawlding Public School

Huan, whose name means *fortunate,* is a fifth grade student at Spawlding Public School. Huan was born and raised in Heshun, a small village in western Yunnan Province, China. He spent the majority of his childhood with his parents, younger brothers, and grandparents in this village. Mandarin, Huan's native language, is spoken in his home. His family immigrated to the West Coast of the United States when Huan was eight years old, and then they moved to the East Coast. At age ten, Huan enrolled as a fourth grader in Spawlding Public School. Schooling in China was quite different in many ways from his experiences in the U.S. In his rural setting, access to special education services was limited and underfunded, so he attended the mainstream classroom. In this setting, he received very few accommodations and class sizes averaged to approximately 40 or 50 students. Rote memorization was the focus of most learning tasks, and respectful, active listening were the norm. Spawlding Public School, in contrast, expects actively engaged learners and class sizes range from 20 to 25 students.

Huan is described by his fifth grade ELA teacher, Kristen, as "a quiet, polite, and motivated student." Huan's social interactions with his peers are age appropriate, and he is attentive and respectful in the classroom. Feng, Huan's younger brother, is eight years old and is in the third grade. Feng has made significant gains in learning the English language and is at an English Language Development Level 3 as compared to Huan who is a Level 1.

Huan was diagnosed with profound sensorineural hearing loss as an infant. At age five, Huan had his first cochlear implant on his right side in China. Huan's cochlear implant dislodged and was re-implanted when his family first moved to a city with excellent hospitals on the West Coast of the United States when Huan was eight. He continued to receive audiological care when his family moved to the town of Spawlding. At Spawlding Medical Center, Huan had a second cochlear implant surgery at age nine on his left side; his processor was activated a few months later. Currently he wears bilateral cochlear N7 processors (see Exhibit A) on both ears for all waking hours.

Huan is an ELL who uses speakers' facial expressions as visual cues to aid his comprehension. He has made some gains in his ability to show more consistent lip-reading/speech-reading skills when interacting with speakers since receiving his second cochlear implant. Nevertheless, Kristen is worried about Huan's ability to engage in grade-level tasks. During morning meetings, for example, Kristen notes that Huan "still opts out completely from participating." She explains, "I usually present a word of the day and ask students to make their own sentences with the word. Today's word was *interpret.* I told the students the definition and then asked them to create original sentences with the word. They engaged in a think-pair-share. Huan never participated in the pair or share."

Results of his Speech & Language Evaluation conducted in September of Grade 5 indicate that Huan has a significant auditory and spoken language disorder, which is most likely secondary to his profound sensorineural hearing impairment. His performance on spoken language assessment tasks present significant deficits in comprehension and expression of Chinese as well as English. He demonstrates inconsistencies in his ability to identify and express labels for many everyday objects and to understand and accurately use prepositions and pronouns. Huan also has difficulty receptively and expressively with verb tenses. Additional information from his WIDA ACCESS® testing reveal the following skill levels (out of 6): Comprehension: 1.8; Reading: 1.8; Listening: 1.8; Writing: 1.8; Literacy: 1.8; Oral: 1.5; Speaking: 1.7; and Overall: 1.8. Huan's ACCESS® results in the L1 range for all skills indicate that he is not yet acquiring English as expected and continues to function as a significantly limited English proficient student.

In September of the fifth grade, Huan's academic abilities were also assessed using several sub-tests from the Woodcock-Johnson IV® (WJ IV) and AIM-Sweb® Curriculum-Based Measurement. The examiner initially presented the test in English but when it was determined that Huan did not understand the directions in English, Huan took the test on a different day when an interpreter could state the directions in Mandarin.

Huan's performance on these tests showed that Huan could identify most letters of the alphabet but struggled to produce the sounds of the letters. Huan read 20 out of 50 sight words and showed his knowledge of the meaning of certain words by pointing to an object when he did not know how to pronounce the word. When pictures were provided as a visual prompt, Huan identified words that corresponded with the pictures. He could write letters in isolation when given the letter orally. Huan had difficulty discriminating between long versus short vowel sounds and voiced and voiceless sounds. He could repeat the sound he heard but, when given a closed set of various sounds, he had difficulty discriminating between them. This is a typical challenge of Chinese learners of English and may be attributed to Huan's L1 interference or his hearing impairment. In math Huan could identify numbers to 500, count to 100 when provided with supports, and add and subtract two-digit numbers.

Presently, Huan attends ESL classes daily. He started fifth grade attending math class with his peers in a general education classroom but, according to Kristen, due to Huan's "significant language deficits and educational disability of sensory impairment," it was determined that he be placed on an individualized education plan and be placed in a pull-out math class with peers and the special education teacher. She says, "Huan is a motivated learner who often relies on his Chinese and/or familiar peers or adults who speak Chinese to understand information."

Kristen asked herself, "What might I do to help support this dually diagnosed learner?" Exhibit B contains a list of supports that she researched on her own. Although having a dually diagnosed learner is intimidating, she is hopeful about supporting him and believes that despite Huan's significant sensory impairment and profound language deficit, when provided with appropriate modifications, he will be given the best outcome for growth and development in literacy (reading and writing) skills in English.

Exhibit A: Overview of Cochlear Implants

A cochlear implant is an electronic device that partially restores hearing. Cochlear implants use a sound processor that fits behind the ear. The processor captures sound signals and transmits them to a receiver implanted under the skin behind the ear. The receiver sends the signals to electrodes implanted in the snail-shaped inner ear. The signals stimulate the auditory nerve, which then directs them to the brain. The brain interprets those signals as sounds, though these sounds won't be just like normal hearing. It takes time and training to learn to interpret the signals received from a cochlear implant. Within a year of use, most people with cochlear implants make considerable gains in understanding speech. (See https://www.mayoclinic.org/tests-procedures/cochlear-implants/about/pac-20385021.)

Exhibit B: Teacher's List of Accommodations

Some accommodations and modifications that would benefit Huan across all settings would be:

- allow continued use of Chinese and promote native language use in the home and during unstructured times with peers to develop native language and help with language transfer.
- provide preferential seating with visual and auditory access to the teacher and peers and away from noise sources (i.e., heating/ac units, hallway noise).
- provide visual cues and repetition.
- provide modeling.
- use of written language to facilitate correct oral language.
- use sentence starters.
- provide small-group oral interaction.
- offer frequent teacher check-ins.
- allow additional time for processing.
- encourage Huan to request definitions of unfamiliar words.
- use visuals and written language for modeling of grammatical corrections orally and in writing.
- create a quiet setting for testing.

I. Pre-Case Discussion Problem Sets

Complete the chart after reading the case.

Facts	
Opinions	
Assumptions	
Theories referred or connected to (if any)	
Ambiguous language	
Criteria you used in analyzing the case (e.g., emotional vs. rational)	
Emerging options	

Write a pre-case discussion decision paper. Include these points:

a. options for case resolution
b. criteria (a rational decision should always be made with a set of criteria)
c. analysis of options
d. recommendation (of the best choice among the options)
e. action plan

II. Case Discussion Questions

Big-Picture Analysis

Describe the context of the case.

- Huan's school and community environment in China vs. the U.S. Inclusive supports at Spawlding Public School

Stakeholders

In small groups, assume the role of one of the case stakeholders. Write a statement/ dialogue expressing this person's or group's hypothetical feelings and perspectives. Be prepared to act out your roles to the large group.

- Huan
- Huan's family
- Kristen
- ESL and special education teachers

Surface Issues

What are the surface issues in this case? What is happening here from an untrained perspective? What underlying assumptions or beliefs feed into this perspective?

Deep Issues

Discuss the real issues in the case. Try to categorize them in terms of language teaching curriculum and instruction.

Evidence-Based Solutions

In groups, develop evidence-based solutions for each deep issue listed. Whenever possible, refer to a theory or principle of language learning and teaching to support your proposed solutions.

Teacher Thinking

In what ways does this case influence and/or reinforce your beliefs and dispositions as a teacher? Consider the Further Reading and Resources section to help with theoretically informed solutions.

III. Post-Case Problem Sets

Post-Case Analysis

A. Categorize what you learned as:
   - teacher knowledge and praxis (e.g., content knowledge, curricular knowledge, pedagogical content knowledge and application)
   - teacher thinking (e.g., beliefs, problem-solving strategies, prioritizing objectives, values, professional ethics, attitudes)

B. List
   - learning objectives that you discovered in the case
   - potential learning outcomes
   - implications for your pedagogical practices

C. The post-case problem sets introduce reactions from various perspectives. These quotes are from others who have read the cases for educational and pedagogical purposes. Read all of the quotes and then choose two quotes about which to write a short response (put the quotes at the top of each response). Use these questions as a guide:
   - What is the message the speaker is trying to convey? If possible, also explain why you chose the quote.
   - What examples can you think of that connect to the themes presented?
   - Can you relate the quote to a class discussion or to something you have read or experienced?

Quotes

1. "This case highlights how teachers cannot do it all alone. How is she supposed to investigate strategies for supporting a learner with significant language and auditory disorders who is hearing impaired and who is learning ESL while supporting the wildly different needs of all students? They don't pay us enough to do what we do. Huan needs everyone on deck to support him and coordinating this is hard."
2. "Although the teacher has little to no experience working with dually diagnosed learners, she has the right disposition and openness to learning new strategies for making learning happen for Huan. She took initiative by conducting initial research on her own. She should reach out to and collaborate with members of the special education and ESL support staff to develop the optimal plan of support. All too often, we as teachers try to do it all alone and that can lead to burnout."

D. Write a reflection describing a take-away from the case in terms of praxis. Make sure to develop an action plan to resolve the case. Consider these questions as guidelines:

- In what ways did the case discussion influence your thinking about the case?
- Did you change your original decision or did the discussion reaffirm your position?
- What points had you not considered prior to the case discussion?
- How might the information you gained from this case be applicable to your current instructional setting and/or future instructional settings?
- What did you learn?
- What are you inspired to learn more about?
- How did the themes discussed in class apply to your experience?

E. Discuss what theoretical basis there is for:

- the stakeholders' behavior in the case.
- the solutions you proposed.

Further Reading and Resources

Gersten, R., & Baker, S. (2003). English language learners with learning disabilities. In H. L. Swanson, K.R. Harris, & S. Graham (Eds.), *Handbook of learning disabilities* (pp. 94–109). New York: Guilford.

Grosjean, F. (2008). The bilingualism and biculturalism of the deaf. *Studying bilinguals*. Oxford, England: Oxford University Press.

Hart, J. E. (2009). Strategies for culturally and linguistically diverse students with special needs. *Preventing School Failure, 53,* 197–203.

Kester, E. (2014). *Difference or disorder: Understanding speech and language patterns in culturally and linguistically diverse students.* Austin, TX: Bilingual Speech and Education Services.

Orosco, M. J., & O'Connor, R. (2014). Culturally responsive instruction for English language learners with disabilities. *Journal of Learning Disabilities, 47,* 515–531.

Paradis, J., Genesee, F., & Crago, M. B. (2010). *Dual language development and disorders: A handbook on bilingualism and second language learning* (2nd ed.). Baltimore: Brookes.

Petitto, L. A., Katerelos, M., Levy, B., Gauna, K., et al. (2001). Bilingual signed and spoken language acquisition from birth: Implications for mechanisms underlying bilingual language acquisition. *Journal of Child Language, 28*(2), 1–44.

Petitto, L. A., & Kovelman, I. (2003, Spring). The bilingual paradox: How signing-speaking bilingual children help us to resolve it and teach us about the brain's mechanisms underlying all language acquisition. *Learning Languages, 8*(3), 5–18.

Yoshinaga-Itano, C., & Sedey, A. (2000). Early speech development in children who are deaf or hard of hearing: Interrelationships with language and hearing. *The Volta Review, 100*(5), 181–211.

3

Cases in Secondary Settings: Inclusive ESL/SEI/TESOL Education

The cases in this chapter span a range of topics in the inclusive education of secondary English learners in traditional ESL and sheltered content-area settings. In the first case, *College First High School*, the teacher needs to support the academic learning and motivation of a student who, in addition to meeting academic goals in a no-excuses, rigorous schooling context, struggles with the socioemotional stresses of the traumatic loss of family from an earthquake in Haiti, his home country. In the second case, *South Bay Middle School*, the reader is asked to analyze the linguistic, educational, and acculturation needs of a reclusive and academically struggling newcomer who is an emergent bilingual learner in a mainstream classroom. In the third case, *Forest Hills High School*, two key themes emerge: distinguishing between learning disability and language difference and differentiating instruction in the mainstream secondary classroom. The cases in this chapter highlight a broad range of pressing topics in the field of secondary English language teaching and learning such as:

- scaffolding approaches to supporting reading and writing development of emerging bilinguals
- supporting the needs of immigrant learners who have experienced trauma, anxiety, and stress and understanding the socioemotional factors that influence language learning

- increasing awareness of inequities in school discipline for emerging bilingual learners of color
- using WIDA language standards and Can Do Descriptors to develop level-appropriate curriculum
- understanding linguistic transfer and interlanguage in student writing
- distinguishing between language acquisition and learning disability in secondary settings and properly identifying processes for special education with English learners
- assessing newcomer students' socioemotional and acculturation needs and promoting an inclusive teaching and learning context
- applying UDL approaches to make content accessible to emerging bilinguals

CASE 3.1

College First High School

"Makenson! You are not tracking me!!" yelled Ms. Thibodeau, a top recruit teacher at College First High School, a no-excuses, discipline-oriented charter school in the Cross Hills school district. The other students murmured and laughed while marching lockstep, with hands by their sides, a school requirement for how they transitioned between classrooms. Refusing to look at the teacher's eyes, or track her, Makenson turned his anger toward his classmates. In a last-ditch effort of defiance, he told another student in line who was laughing to "shut up." Ms. Thibodeau immediately responded, "Get out and go to the dean's office immediately. You are out of line and you failed to track me when asked; this is a violation of community rules. Now go!"

The teachers at College First High School are all working to help the district to meet the Adequate Yearly Progress goals. Exhibit A provides an overview of the student achievement data for the district. The emphasis on obedience at College First is believed to equip its students—the majority of whom face socioeconomic barriers to success—for college and career readiness. Exhibit B highlights key demographic data. The school offers a rigorous, college-prep, curriculum, a longer school day, and a disciplinarian approach. The school celebrates its success of high test scores by minority students on statewide tests; this bolsters their confidence in the success of their no-excuses model. Recently, the state has required that schools offer equitable educational opportunities for ELLs and include and disaggregate the test scores of ELLs on statewide tests. The number of ELLs has steadily increased at College First. Makenson, who enrolled in College First High two years ago, is one of these emerging bilingual learners. Although the school claims to embrace inclusive supports for ELLs in the mainstream classroom, the reality is that none of the teachers, including Ms. Thibodeau, have any training in or experiences with English language learning and teaching.

Ms. Thibodeau's ELA class comprised 15 students, 3 of whom were ELLs. In her most recent lesson, Ms. Thibodeau started the class right away, without any framing, and showed *Macbeth*. She said to the students, "Stop the talking. Remember, you can track along with your book as we watch." Most students did just that, but Makenson spun the book around on his desk, chatted with peers, and fidgeted around during the entire 20-minute film.

During an informal lunch meeting with the grade-level dean and principal about Makenson, Ms. Thibodeau explained, "Students are required to keep still and have their hands folded on the desks during instructional time. Makenson, by contrast, fidgets around and distracts his peers with busyness and foolishness." She continued, "I have attended universal design training. I am making the lesson accessible by providing subtitles and summarizing the video throughout. He refuses to participate despite my efforts to scaffold. Makenson is totally defiant and lacks age-appropriate social skills. He is a major disruption in my day-to-day lessons. We have to consider expulsion. We just cannot support this student."

After the line-transition incident with Ms. Thibodeau and Makenson's subsequent dismissal to the dean's office, the new academic dean, Mrs. McCarthy, asked Makenson to share his perspective. Mrs. McCarthy is the first African-American administrator at College First, with more than 15 years of educational leadership and teaching experience, which began with her work in low socioeconomic status communities in New Orleans after Hurricane Katrina.

Mrs. McCarthy greeted Makenson with a warm smile, the first he had received from an authority figure since he arrived at this school. "They want me to behave like a robot. They look down on me, both the teachers and the students," explained Makenson. "Sometimes it is hard for me to understand what the teacher says. I did not understand or see why the *Macbeth* video was important. I was confused about what to do." Feeling like he was finally being heard by Mrs. McCarthy, Makenson opened up about the trauma he experienced after losing all of his family in the Haiti earthquake and began to cry. He explained that he moved here to live with his uncle after his parents and siblings were killed in the earthquake. Mrs. McCarthy asked Makenson if he was hungry. "Yes," he replied. He told her he often doesn't have breakfast. He seemed to perk up and engage more in the conversation after eating the granola bar.

After talking with Makenson, Mrs. McCarthy requested a formal meeting with the grade-level dean, Ms. Thibodeau, and the principal. She explained,

"In my perspective, ELLs in College First High struggle to balance the rigorous demands associated with simultaneously acquiring English and mastering content in various disciplines. In addition to these enormous cognitive demands, other factors—such as issues associated with living in low socioeconomic conditions and difficulties integrating into a new culture—contribute to the persistent academic achievement gap that disproportionately affects ELLs in College First High. As the data reveal, we are failing our English learners. We need to learn specific strategies for supporting the language, acculturation, and socio-emotional needs of English learners within our curriculum. Although UDL is a general strategy for all learners, perhaps there are ways you can infuse tailored supports to engage and support the inclusion and access for students like Makenson."

Ms. Thibodeau replied, "I know this may sound heartless, but there is no room in the rigorous curriculum to support the socioemotional needs of English learners. I expect these students to abide by the basic expectations for behavior and respect. He does not do that. What about my socioemotional needs as a teacher? I give all of my students scaffolding and tailored instruction through my UDL strategies. This student simply refuses to participate and respect community rules. I am not a guidance counselor. I am a teacher. "

The grade-level dean joined in the conversation: "I agree that we cannot afford to support the needs of students like Makenson. We all integrate UDL strategies. I use visuals, for example. He simply chooses to defy basic instructions. Maybe he would be better served in the public school system."

Mrs. McCarthy knew she was an outlier amid a status-quo culture and teachers who dismissed whole-child support for ELLs like Makenson. It was clear that they wanted him to face expulsion as this was the third time this month he had been sent to the dean's office. Still, given her history with students who have experienced trauma, Mrs. McCarthy chose to speak up: "It's of grave concern to me that ELLs, along with students with disabilities, face more expulsions from school. Your prioritization of academic achievement seems to come at such a high cost."

Exhibit C features the school's most recent discipline and retention data.

An uncomfortable silence settled in the room as the decision about Makenson's future hung in the balance.

Exhibit A: Statewide Achievement Data

Data from statewide tests show that the achievement gap continues to disproportionately affect ELLs at College First. Of all the ELLs and former ELLs in the district, 64 percent failed or needed improvement in ELA, 56 percent failed or needed improvement in math, and 75 percent failed or needed improvement in science. At the high school level, statewide test scores are persistently low for ELLs. Of the ninth grade ELLs and former ELLs, 56 percent failed or needed improvement in English language arts and 43 percent failed or needed improvement in math.

Exhibit B: Demographic Data

The majority of ELLs who attend College First live at or below the poverty line, and most receive free or reduced lunch. In the school, 54 percent of the student population receives free lunch and 8.6 percent receives reduced lunch. Overall, 62.6 percent of the student population in College First High is considered low income.

Most ELLs in the school are first-generation immigrants. Many of these students have had interrupted formal schooling experiences and some are not literate in their home language. A large number of ELLs come from single-parent households. Of all current ELLs in the school, 13.4 percent of the students are in sheltered English immersion (SEI) classrooms and 47.6 percent are in what the school refers to as SEI 2 classrooms for ELL students with high-intermediate or advanced English language proficiency.

Retention and Discipline

The data on discipline reveals that African-American and Latinx students at College First High School were disciplined at a 70 percent higher rate than their white peers. ELLs have the highest dropout rates of all student groups, averaging 5 percent annually.

I. Pre-Case Discussion Problem Sets

Complete the chart after reading the case.

Facts	
Opinions	
Assumptions	
Theories referred or connected to (if any)	
Ambiguous language	
Criteria you used in analyzing the case (e.g., emotional vs. rational)	
Emerging options	

Write a pre-case discussion decision paper. Include these points:

a. options for case resolution
b. criteria (a rational decision should always be made with a set of criteria)
c. analysis of options
d. recommendation (of the best choice among the options)
e. action plan

II. Case Discussion Questions

Big-Picture Analysis

Describe the context of the case.

- student demographic information
- school educational model
- retention and achievement data

Stakeholders

In small groups, assume the role of one of the case stakeholders. Write a statement/ dialogue expressing this person's or group's hypothetical feelings and perspectives. Be prepared to act out your roles to the large group.

- Makenson
- Ms. Thibodeau
- Mrs. McCarthy, Academic Dean
- school principal
- grade-level dean

Surface Issues

What are the surface issues in this case? What is happening here from an untrained perspective? What underlying assumptions or beliefs feed into this perspective?

Deep Issues

Discuss the real issues in the case. Try to categorize them in terms of language teaching curriculum and instruction.

Evidence-Based Solutions

In groups, develop evidence-based solutions for each deep issue listed. Whenever possible, refer to a theory or principle of language learning and teaching to support your proposed solutions.

Teacher Thinking

In what ways does this case influence and/or reinforce your beliefs and dispositions as a teacher? Consult the Further Readings and Resources section to help with theoretically informed solutions.

III. Post-Case Problem Sets

Post-Case Analysis

A. Categorize what you learned as:
   - teacher knowledge and praxis (e.g., content knowledge, curricular knowledge, pedagogical content knowledge and application)
   - teacher thinking (e.g., beliefs, problem-solving strategies, prioritizing objectives, values, professional ethics, attitudes)

B. List:
   - learning objectives that you discovered in the case
   - potential learning outcomes
   - implications for your pedagogical practices

C. The post-case problem sets introduce reactions from various perspectives. These quotes are from others who have read the cases for educational and pedagogical purposes. Read all of the quotes and then choose two quotes about which to write a short response (put the quotes at the top of each response). Use these questions as a guide:
   - What is the message the speaker is trying to convey? If possible, also explain why you chose the quote.
   - What examples can you think of that connect to the themes presented?
   - Can you relate the quote to a class discussion or to something you have read or experienced?

Quotes

1. "The entire culture of the no-excuses school is too harsh for students like Makenson. The strange cult-like culture within a culture including the school language like 'track me' is probably overwhelming for students like him. The hyperstrict disciplinary environment where stillness is prized ahead of active learning is counter to inclusive teaching."
2. "Students like Makenson are highly disruptive. It is good that the academic dean is there to figure this situation out, because the teacher has the duty to be responsible for the rest of the students who actually want to learn."
3. "This case highlights how important it is to consider research on motivation and language learning. After losing family members in an earthquake and needing to transition here to a new context as an adolescent and adapt to a new language and learning context, schooling and life is probably all very overwhelming. Has the teacher done any research on the learner's background?"

D. Write a reflection describing a take-away from the case in terms of praxis. Make sure to develop an action plan to resolve the case. Consider these questions as guidelines:

- In what ways did the case discussion influence your thinking about the case?
- Did you change your original decision or did the discussion reaffirm your position?
- What points had you not considered prior to the case discussion?
- How might the information you gained from this case be applicable to your current instructional setting and/or future instructional settings?
- What did you learn?
- What are you inspired to learn more about?
- How did the themes discussed in class apply to your experience?

E. Discuss what theoretical basis there is for:

- the stakeholders' behaviors in the case.
- the solutions you proposed.

Further Reading and Resources

Artiga, S., & Ubri, P. (2017, December). Living in an immigrant family in America: How fear and toxic stress are affecting daily life, well-being, & health. Retrieved from www.kff.org/racial-equity-and-health-policy/issue-brief/living-in-an-immigrant-family-in-america-how-fear-and-toxic-stress-are-affecting-daily-life-well-being-health/

Blaustein, M. E. (2013). Childhood trauma and a framework for intervention. In E. Rossen & R. Hull (Eds.), *Supporting and educating traumatized students: A guide for school-based professionals* (pp. 3–22). New York: Oxford University Press.

Colorín Colorado. (2018). How to provide socioemotional support for immigrant students. Retrieved from https://www.colorincolorado.org/immigration/guide/student

Dillard, C. (2018). School-to-deportation pipeline. *Teaching Tolerance, 60,* 42–45. Retrieved from https://www.tolerance.org/magazine/fall-2018

Duval, S. (2017). Antiracist practices: Strengthening students' sense of self to promote hope and confidence for student success. In S. Wong, E. Sánchez Gosnell, A. M. Foerster Luu, & L. Dodson (Eds.), *Teachers as allies: Transformative practices for teaching DREAMers & undocumented students* (pp. 45-58). New York: Teachers College Press.

Hart, R. (2009). Child refugees, trauma and education: Interactionist considerations on social and emotional needs and development. *Educational Psychology in Practice, 25*(4), 351–368.

Kubota, R., & Lin, A. (2009). *Race, class, identity in second language education: Exploring critically engaged practice.* New York: Routledge.

Lippi-Green, R. (2012). *English with an accent: Language ideology and discrimination in the United States.* New York: Routledge.

Niehaus, K., & Adelson, J. L. (2014). School support, parental involvement, and academic and socioemotional outcomes for English language learners. *American Educational Research Journal, 51*(4), 810–844.

Ralabate, P., & Nelson, L. (2017). *Culturally responsive design for English language learners: The UDL approach.* Wakefield, MA: CAST Professional Publishing.

Shim, J. (2017). Self-identified linguistic microaggressions among monolingual preservice teachers: Why they matter for English language learners. *Multicultural Learning and Teaching, 12*(2). doi.org/10.1515/mlt-2016-0017

Torres, C., & Rao, K. (2019). *UDL for language learners.* Wakefield, MA: CAST Professional Publishing.

Skiba, R. Mediratta, K., & Rausch, M. (2016). *Inequality in school discipline: Research and practice to reduce disparities.* New York: Palgrave Macmillian.

Soures, K., & Hall, P. (2016). *Fostering resilient learners: Strategies for creating a trauma-sensitive classroom.* Alexandria, VA: ASCD Publishing.

Zacarain, D., Alvarez-Ortiz, L., & Haynes, J. (2017). *Teaching to strengths: Supporting students living with trauma, violence, and chronic stress.* Alexandria, VA: ACSD.

CASE 3.2

South Bay Middle School

Mariana came to the United States two years ago with her family from Bogotá, Colombia, where she says she had "a very happy and good life." The weather was very warm, the food was healthy and delicious (even at her school), and the atmosphere in her home and school environment was full of *cariño (*tender-loving care), a sharp contrast from what she explains she is experiencing here in the United States as a sixth grade student enrolled in South Bay Middle School.

Mariana attended private school in Colombia and told her teacher that "school is quite different in Colombia." She did not have to take double math and double literacy blocks, and there was more time for arts, music, and free play. Mariana is very worried because back home she had many friends and was "popular"; moreover, she often played with her friends outside for hours after school and on weekends. She has cried to her mother, "*Mami, no tengo amigos aquí*" (I don't have friends here). Spanish is the only language spoken in her home.

A typical day meandering the dark hallways with unfamiliar faces and difficulty understanding language makes life at school less joyful for Mariana than it was back home where she could easily converse with teachers and friends. She feels desperate to make human connections, but after three months in this school, Mariana often walks around with her head down low, hoping to blend in and terrified that someone will make fun of her broken English.

The teachers are very concerned about Mariana's academic progress and lack of engagement in school and are considering a special education evaluation. Her math and ELA teachers, Kellyann and Jenn, have called for a special education referral meeting to discuss their concerns. Kellyann, who was raised in rural Pennsylvania and educated in a primarily culturally homogenous university, thinks that "just good teaching" will help all learners thrive. This is her first teaching job. During her teacher education program, she was never required to take a course on meeting the needs of English learners in math. "There is very little language in math, aside from word problems. Mariana struggles with basic formulaic knowledge, unlike my other English learners," said Kellyann. She showed her colleagues the "simple" math problem that Mariana left blank as evidence of her concerns with Mariana's cognitive development. Although Kellyann spent every day after school reviewing math concepts with Mariana, she still was unable to complete the following math problem: Jackie made a jack o' lantern. She scooped out two pounds of pulp. If the pumpkin weighed seven pounds at the beginning, how much does it weigh now?

During the pre-initial referral meeting, Mariana's teachers and dean discussed their concerns. "Her comprehension is low and her expressive skills are poor. She is not making satisfactory progress in any of her content courses. I think we need to consider an evaluation," asserted Kellyann. "I agree," said Mariana's history teacher. "She seems to be lost in my social studies class, even though she is partnered with another Spanish-speaking peer." The part-time ELL Coordinator noted that they could not rule out language-based needs without providing an appropriate intervention. Exhibit A includes the observation notes emailed to teachers from the ELL Coordinator's first observation of Mariana in the classroom context. It includes suggestions for scaffolding language and learning. In addition, she provided a handout of WIDA Can Do Descriptors (https://wida.wisc.edu/sites/default/files/resource/CanDo-KeyUses-Gr-6-8.pdf). The teachers thought that what Mariana really needed was one-on-one ESL instruction, which they did not have the time to provide in their content courses as it would slow the pace of the lesson. Realizing that none of the teachers in the school have ESL licensure or training, the ELL Coordinator tried to quickly summarize some go-to strategies that would make content accessible in the classroom. She also emphasized that her own caseload was "up to the max" and simply could not take on another student. She stated, "Something must be done. You have to implement these strategies, develop a plan for language goals, and we can come back and discuss her progress in six weeks, ok?" The ELL Coordinator left the meeting hurriedly and bid the teachers "good luck" as she rushed off to another meeting at another school in the district.

Frustrated on her way home, the ELL Coordinator called the superintendent of schools: "I have been telling you for the past two years that we need to have certified English language teachers at each school. I cannot meet the needs of individual students, attend education plan referral meetings, conduct WIDA evaluations, provide professional development for teachers, and conduct coaching and observations for five schools in your district at 12 hours a week. At some point, the fact that we are not providing adequate supports for our limited English proficient learners is going to be reflected in your prized schoolwide data." Exhibit B contains portions of the letter the ELL Coordinator sent to the superintendent two years before this meeting; it never received a response.

In Mariana's current sixth grade social studies classroom, 26 students sit in rows of three. The teacher has strategically seated her next to her "buddy" who is supposed to provide native language support during content discussions. However, Mariana has reported to her mother that the buddy spoke very little conversational Spanish and could barely translate even one vocabulary word in her content-area classes. She struggled to understand what the teachers say in classes because of her limited English and she often disengages.

Mariana recently transitioned to the school from another district. Unfortunately, the district did not provide any information about Mariana's English language developmental level or include any documents (e.g., a home language survey). The ELL Coordinator reached out to the district ELL coordinator from Mariana's previous school setting, with no response for more than two months. Upon informally assessing Mariana's reading skills using a W-APT screener, an initial English language proficiency assessment used to identify ELLs, the ELL Coordinator told the other teachers, "I would assess her as a limited English proficient learner who is probably at a Level 2 overall. In terms of reading a sixth grade text, she was able to decode and comprehend the basic gist of the story but was not able to retell a summary in English due to her limited vocabulary. She needs support comprehending Tier 2 and Tier 3 words and would benefit from background building pre-reading activities." The ELA teacher replied, "Can you say what that means in English?" The other teachers laughed. The ELL Coordinator once again pointed the teachers to the Can Do Descriptors and explained that this will be a great starting point for learning about tailored supports. The ELA teacher replied, "Um, can you say what that means in English?" Again, there was laughter. The ELL Coordinator once again pointed them to the Can Do Descriptors and told them they should just "experiment with stuff to see what works."

During a typical social studies class, Mariana's teacher begins with a "Do Now" question that is written on the overhead projector. He prides himself on using the PowerPoint slide to make the question visual. This day's question was, "Explain how modern governments can trace some of their attributes to the systems of power, authority, and governance established in ancient civilizations." Mariana wrote one sentence: "Gubernments has power and authority on ancient civilizations cause money."

Exhibit A: Observation Notes and Recommendations for Teachers from the ELL Coordinator

Mariana's receptive skills are stronger than her expressive skills so be sure to provide sentence frames, vocabulary banks, and alternative means of participation (e.g., pointing, labeling, illustrating) to show what she understands. Therefore, it is recommended that teachers refer to the WIDA Can Do Descriptors for Grades 6–8 (https://wida.wisc.edu/sites/default/files/resource/CanDo-Booklet-Gr-6-8.pdf) to identify what Mariana is able to do well with instructional support in the classroom. She has a buddy assigned to her in classes but she explained to me that the scholar's Spanish is not really proficient, making the translation challenging. Perhaps we could equip the student and their teachers with the SayHi translator app to assist her comprehension and participation. In addition, we have Rosetta Stone and would like to have her use this weekly (e.g., Thursdays) to build her basic functional English skills. I have attached a book of strategies that support language development across the four domains (Reading, Writing, Listening, and Speaking).

Exhibit B: Letter to Superintendent

Dear Superintendent Whitter:

In the current context, with a lack of a certified teacher for English learners on-site and teachers with no formative training on scaffolding for ELLs, English learners are *not* receiving the accommodations, supports, and differentiation that will help them access and engage with grade-level content. The Leveled Literacy Intervention (LLI) system and Response to Intervention (RTI) interventions are not intentionally designed to target the specific language developmental needs of English learners. Although the LLI intervention is generally effective for struggling readers and probably helpful for ELLs, it still does not (a) build background knowledge, (b) front-load and recycle Tier 1, 2 (high-frequency, multiple meaning) and 3 (high-level, technical) vocabulary, (c) integrate the four domains of language and address the oral and aural language domain developmental needs, (d) promote higher-order thinking skills (or HOTS), and (e) differentiate supports and language objectives according to English language proficiency levels. Students who are designated English learners must receive targeted linguistic support in order to make content comprehensible.

Recommendations

Ideally, the educational leadership team and staff would very much appreciate comprehensive training on sheltered English instruction. However, budget and costs are a concern. The principal and director of special education would like me to present a session for professional development for teachers during their August training. There should be at least one teacher per grade-level cohort in attendance. Teachers need support in infusing task-based instruction to support writing accuracy. They need to learn the importance of pre-teaching and recycling vocabulary and creating and incorporating language objectives. Moreover, they would benefit from a review of content-specific strategies in math and science. Parental engagement is an additional concern. Multilingual parent education events and strategies for teachers on effectively communicating with families of ELLs is strongly recommended to boost home-school connections.

I. Pre-Case Discussion Problem Sets

Complete the chart after reading the case.

Facts	
Opinions	
Assumptions	
Theories referred or connected to (if any)	
Ambiguous language	
Criteria you used in analyzing the case (e.g., emotional vs. rational)	
Emerging options	

Write a pre-case discussion decision paper. Include these points:

a. options for case resolution
b. criteria (a rational decision should always be made with a set of criteria)
c. analysis of options
d. recommendation (of the best choice among the options)
e. action plan

II. Case Discussion Questions

Big-Picture Analysis

Describe the context of the case.

- student's current and former learning context
- SEI in mainstream

Stakeholders

In small groups, assume the role of one of the case stakeholders. Write a statement/ dialogue expressing this person's or group's hypothetical feelings and perspectives. Be prepared to act out your roles to the large group.

- Mariana
- Kellyann and Jenn
- ELL Coordinator
- Mariana's peer buddy
- principal
- other grade-level teachers

Surface Issues

What are the surface issues in this case? What is happening here from an untrained perspective? What underlying assumptions or beliefs feed into this perspective?

Deep Issues

Discuss the real issues in the case. Try to categorize them in terms of language teaching curriculum and instruction.

Evidence-Based Solutions

In groups, develop evidence-based solutions for each deep issue listed. Whenever possible, refer to a theory or principle of language learning and teaching to support your proposed solutions.

Teacher Thinking

In what ways does this case influence and/or reinforce your beliefs and dispositions as a teacher? Consult the Further Readings and Resources section to help with theoretically informed solutions.

III. Post-Case Problem Sets

Post-Case Analysis

A. Categorize what you learned as:
- teacher knowledge and praxis (e.g., content knowledge, curricular knowledge, pedagogical content knowledge and application)
- teacher thinking (e.g., beliefs, problem-solving strategies, prioritizing objectives, values, professional ethics, attitudes)

B. List:
- learning objectives that you discovered in the case
- potential learning outcomes
- implications for your pedagogical practices

C. The post-case problem sets introduce reactions from various perspectives. These quotes are from others who have read the cases for educational and pedagogical purposes. Read all of the quotes and then choose two quotes about which to write a short response (put the quotes at the top of each response). Use these questions as a guide:
- What is the message the speaker is trying to convey? If possible, also explain why you chose the quote.
- What examples can you think of that connect to the themes presented?
- Can you relate the quote to a class discussion or to something you have read or experienced?

Quotes

1. "This case points out the utter failure of schools to fulfill the English-only model of instruction. This student is left to sink or swim, literally, and the teachers are not instituting any appropriate language scaffolds to make learning accessible to Mariana."
2. "The collectivistic and individualistic school learning contexts in Colombia vs. the U.S. must be very challenging for this young learner to navigate. Couple that with adolescence and it is a recipe for disaster for her unless someone intervenes. It seems like no one is responsible to support her acculturation needs."
3. "The math teacher fails to see the embedded and culturally based vocabulary items in the word problems. Even math contains difficult language that can pose a challenge to emerging bilingual learners."
4. "I don't think the teachers can do much more for this student, and there is no time to waste. Without a certified ESL teacher on site, they need to give her some level of support, so special education is better than nothing. There is no way a teacher would be able to provide her with the level of scaffolded writing and reading instruction in the mainstream classroom without disrupting her overall teaching."

D. Write a reflection describing a take-away from the case in terms of praxis. Make sure to develop an action plan to resolve the case. Consider these questions as guidelines:

- In what ways did the case discussion influence your thinking about the case?
- Did you change your original decision or did the discussion reaffirm your position?
- What points had you not considered prior to the case discussion?
- How might the information you gained from this case be applicable to your current instructional setting and/or future instructional settings?
- What did you learn?
- What are you inspired to learn more about?
- How did the themes discussed in class apply to your experience?

E. Discuss what theoretical basis there is for:

- the stakeholders' behavior in the case.
- the solutions you proposed.

Further Reading and Resources

Calderón, M. (2004). *Standards-based writing for English language learners*. Los Angeles: Los Angeles County Office of Education.

Durgunoğlu, A. Y. (2002). Cross-linguistic transfer in literacy development and implications for language learners. *Annals of Dyslexia, 52,* 189–204.

Lawrence, M. (2015). *How to support the socioemotional of middle/high school ELLs.* Retrieved from https://www.colorincolorado.org/article/social-and-emotional-needs-middle-and-high-school-ells

Marshall, H., & DeCapua, A. (2013). *Making the transition to classroom success: Culturally responsive teaching for struggling language learners.* Ann Arbor: University of Michigan Press.

Niehaus, K., & Adelson, J. L. (2014). School support, parental involvement, and academic and socioemotional outcomes for English language learners. *American Educational Research Journal, 51*(4), 810–844.

Paris, D., & Alim, H. S. (2014). What are we seeking to sustain through culturally sustaining pedagogy? A loving critique forward. *Harvard Educational Review, 84*(1), 85–100.

Richard-Amato, P., & Snow, M. (2004). *Academic success for English language learners: Strategies for K–12 mainstream teachers.* Boston: Pearson.

Suárez-Orozco, C., Pimentel, A., & Martin, M. (2009). The significance of relationships. Academic engagement and achievement among newcomer immigrant youth. *Teachers College Record, 111*(3), 712–749.

Suárez-Orozco, C., Rhodes, J., & Milburn, M. (2009). Unraveling the immigrant paradox: Academic engagement and disengagement among recently arrived immigrant youth. *Youth & Society, 41*(2), 151–185.

Suárez-Orozco, C., & Suárez-Orozco, M. M. (2001). *Children of immigration.* Cambridge, MA: Harvard University Press.

WIDA. (2012). English language proficiency standards. www.wida.edu

Wright, W. E. (2010). *Foundations for teaching English Language Learners: Research, theory, policy, and practice.* Philadelphia: Caslon Publishing.

Zacarain, D., Alvarez-Ortiz, L., & Haynes, J. (2017). *Teaching to strengths: Supporting students living with trauma, violence, and chronic stress.* Alexandria, VA: ACSD.

Zwiers, J. (2008). *Building academic language. Essential practices for content classrooms. Grades 5–12.* San Francisco: Jossey-Bass Publishers.

CASE 3.3

Forest Hills High School

Forest Hills High School is located ten miles west of a city in the northeastern part of the United States. The 1,500 students at this comprehensive high school have myriad pportunities to be involved in their learning through career and technical education pathways, the fine and performing arts, STEM electives, athletics, and more. In the last ten years, Forest Hills has seen a significant increase in its English learner population. An overwhelming number of English learners in the district are undocumented students who arrive on their own (separated from their parents) from Guatemala and are living with aunts or cousins. Many of these students have to work after school so that they can send remittances back home to family members, so teachers report that homework for them is out of the question as it never gets done.

Until last year, Forest Hills did not have a qualified ELL Coordinator on-site. Instead, all "at risk" cases went directly to the Special Education Department. The ESL teacher, Betty, provided all newcomers with ESL instruction for about an hour a day; for the rest of the day, these students were placed in mainstream classes to sink or swim. Betty feels strongly that the system is broken and that ELs in Forest Hills are not receiving the support they need to access grade-level content. "It is impossible for me to fill the language gaps needed for their success in the mainstream classroom. Some of these kids cannot even write a complete sentence and they are in twelfth grade," she explained.

Mr. Richard, the school principal, has been a Forest Hills resident his entire life. He has worked in this leadership position for more than 20 years. He knew something had to be done to better support the growing population of ELs in the district, so he subcontracted an ELL Coordinator to investigate opportunities for improved schooling for ELLs.

The following findings were a result of a qualitative investigation of English language support at Forest Hills High School conducted by Ann, then externally contracted ELL Coordinator, after spending two months in the school:

> One overarching theme that emerged from my interviews with the special education team, mainstream teachers, and observations was the overrepresentation of English learners in special education in the high school. In the past few months alone, there have been 11 special educa-

tion referral cases, all of which are ELs. The special education team has voiced specific concerns about the education plan referral criteria not aligning with state special education mandates. One common question is why students who score under 40 percent on STAR™ (see Exhibit A) are referred for RTI (Response to Intervention) when it should be under 25 percent so kids with the most need get identified, not just ELs who may have some gaps in language. Thus, a major ethical concern is the high number of ELs in special education when the team expressed what they really need is English language push-in or sheltered support in the classroom. This finding was confirmed in my memo notes based on observations.

There are many missed opportunities for scaffolded learning for ELs in the classroom. In my interviews with teachers, they are eager to support the needs of ELs but feel ill-equipped to do so. I have been meeting with grade-level cohorts to address this need and suggest ways to make content comprehensible to ELs with varying proficiency levels. There are a few cases of ELs who would be categorized as LEP who need support for their English language proficiency level.. When I arrived, these students were unable to engage in grade-level tasks and they were not receiving English language level-appropriate supports.

There are many cases of ELs who are exhibiting disruptive behavior and inattention which, based on my observations, could likely be due to their lack of comprehension of and accessibility to the content. Nevertheless, in the current context, with a lack of an EL certified teacher coach on-site and teachers with no formative training on scaffolding for ELs, these students are not receiving the accommodations, supports, and differentiation that will help them access and engage with grade-level content.

The LLI and RTI interventions are not intentionally designed to target the specific language developmental needs of English learners. Although the LLI intervention is generally effective for struggling readers and probably helpful for ELs, it still does not (a) build background knowledge, (b) front-load and recycle Tier 1, 2, and 3 vocabulary, (c) integrate the four domains of language and address the oral and aural language domain developmental needs, (d) promote higher-order thinking skills (HOTS), and (e) differentiate supports and language objectives according to English language proficiency levels.

Ann delivered the report to Mr. Richard and firmly expressed that something had to drastically change. She provided the report in the hopes that the teachers would receive more training professional development opportunities on scaffolding and differentiated language teaching and learning. Mr. Richard thanked Ann for her work and told her that she was contracted for another three months to provide one-on-one coaching for teachers. No mention of the report or Ann's findings were made to anyone else, and there was no indication that Mr. Richard took into consideration any of Ann's recommendations. Ann felt that her presence was there mainly as a Band-Aid.

Problems continued to plague the school as mainstream teachers, with little to no training in teaching English learners, would grapple with decisions about how to best support their English learners.

One student who recently was brought to Ann's attention is Rodrigo, an undocumented Guatemalan-born high school student who has been in the U.S. for three years. His ninth grade ELA teacher, Christina, asked Ann to observe him in class.

"I would like to request that you observe and maybe assess Rodrigo as part of his special education referral," expressed Christina. "I am quite concerned about his ability to concentrate despite distraction, boredom, or fatigue. Concentration is a skill that requires a lot of self-discipline and I speak to him about this almost weekly, especially during independent reading. I ask him constantly to focus on classroom tasks no matter what is going on around him but I always catch him wandering away. Do you know any strategies of how I can help him to deal effectively with intrusive thoughts?"

Ann subsequently observed Rodrigo and tooks notes on three occasions (see Exhibit B) and provided a set of tailored recommendations (see Exhibit C).

Exhibit A: The STAR™ Reading Assessment

Developed by Renaissance Learning, the STAR™ Reading assessment is a comprehensive examination that tests the range of students' knowledge of reading and language. Questions on this test cover 46 reading-skill areas spread across five domains. Reading domains include analyzing literary text, word skills and knowledge, analyzing argument and evaluating text, comprehension strategies and constructing meaning, and understanding author's craft.

The STAR Reading™ assessment is used by educators to identify students' strengths and areas of need in reading and offers specific insight into which areas need improvement. Data from this assessment is also used to inform instruction, monitor students' progress, and pinpoint whether or not students are meeting the expectations of state standards.

Exhibit B: ELL Coordinator Observation Notes of Rodrigo in Mainstream Classes

Observation #1

The math class goal was that the scholars calculated the volume of right rectangular prisms. The teacher had the lesson content objectives posted. Rodrigo completed all of the fluency and packet work on time without difficulty. He chose not to participate in physical activity designed to give his brain a break (lunges and other activities); you can see he wanted to but perhaps was embarrassed due to lack of knowledge of key fitness words such as *lunge, freeze, knee up,* etc. There was a fluency test, and it was all numerical (no written directions). Therefore, he completed the work effortlessly and expeditiously compared to peers. He was able to follow the teacher's simple, single-step directions but seemed to struggle with more complex directions and language. Throughout the duration of the 40-minute observation, the student appeared to be attentive, focused, and on task.

Observation #2

Rodrigo has preferential seating. After independent reading of the text, the scholars were supposed to engage in a "Do Now" quick-write writing activity. This was a text-based question about *The Odyssey* that was projected on the slide:

> Do Now Question:
>
> *Think about what you know about Odysseus' character now. What do you learn of him after he loses six men to Scylla? Have you ever seen him boastful or confident? Cite textual evidence in your response.*

While all of the other students were writing, the scholar shuffled his notebook and rubbed his eyes for the first three minutes. With two-and-a-half minutes remaining, the teacher helped to direct scholar. By the end of the journal time, he began to write one sentence, while his peers had all written paragraphs with textual evidence to support their opinion. He wrote: "Odyseus' caracter no good an good sometime."

After the "Do Now," the teacher asked students to orally share what they had written as a whole group. In her effort to include Rodrigo, she called on him first. Blushing, he hesitated to respond and ultimately chose to be silent. The teacher asked three other students who provided detailed answers for which they received praise. Then the teacher shifted gears to vocabulary review. She asks students to repeat the pronunciation of the word *morbid*, but Rodrigo did not follow this direction. The words were not written anywhere.

Christina, his teacher, reported, "He doesn't respond to simple directions, like when the teacher asks students to give a thumbs-up if the word has a positive connotation or a thumbs-down for negative." The teacher used visuals and an integrated approach to vocabulary instruction. When asking students about what parts of speech the words are, he was rubbing his eyes. The teacher tried to redirect him, but he didn't seem to focus as he was staring at ceiling. The teacher then asked students to engage in a turn-and-talk to interpret word meaning. He was unable to share information with friends but listened to peers. The teacher used a great rephrasing strategy at this point and asked the scholar to summarize what his peers said. For the next turn-and-talk, when it was time for the stop and jot, he actually was the first to share with a colleague. It is suggested that this opportunity to think/write and then pair-share is effective. Also, teacher redirection is a helpful strategy. Throughout the rest of the lesson, his participation and engagement waxes and waned. He often looked up at the ceiling. I wonder what the teachers might have done or do to make the text more accessible.

Observation #3

During the independent reading period, Rodrigo was engaged some of the time with the text but was often distracted and would need to be redirected compared to his peers. Perhaps the text was at a level beyond his comprehensibility. Or, perhaps, he would benefit from scaffolding of the text to make it more accessible.

Following the observations, Christina met with Ann. Christina noted that she was instituting some scaffolds for Rodrigo, but Ann insisted that it was not enough. Ann told Christina that she would start to institute a set of tailored supports for Rodrigo to rule out language as a barrier to learning and potential cause for his inattentiveness. Ann requested that Christina support his writing and reading comprehension with a suite of supports (see Exhibit C) and then meet every six weeks for two cycles to discuss Rodrigo's progress. Christina smiled and then went into the lunchroom to complain to her colleague. She exclaimed, "Sarah, I am tired of these outsiders coming in and telling us what our kids need. I have spent two months with Rodrigo and two years in this school. I can tell a focus and attention problem when I see one. Now he is going to miss out on the support he really needs because some know-it-all doctor who probably hasn't ever taught in a real school wants to tell me it could be a language problem."

Exhibit C: ELL Coordinator's Recommended Language Supports for Rodrigo

Recommendations

- Rodrigo should continue to have frequent check-ins with the teacher.
- Provide Rodrigo with modified texts, texts with annotations, texts with visuals, and/or audio text if the core text is above his reading level.
- If during checks for understanding, scholar shows difficulty understanding, provide opportunities to re-teach, explain, or partner him with a student who demonstrates strong understanding.
- Rodrigo would benefit from background building and activation of prior knowledge activities prior to each lesson.
- Rodrigo will access the content better with instructional scaffolding of Tier 2 (high-frequency, multiple meaning) and 3 (high-level, technical) vocabulary and multiple opportunities to interact with and be exposed to new words.
- Rodrigo should be thoughtfully paired with other students based on language readiness and levels, as well as language modeling opportunities.
- Encourage scholar to repeat and rephrase directions and continue to give clear, multi-step directions.
- Make directions aural and visual whenever possible.

I. Pre-Case Discussion Problem Sets

Complete the chart after reading the case.

Facts	
Opinions	
Assumptions	
Theories referred or connected to (if any)	
Ambiguous language	
Criteria you used in analyzing the case (e.g., emotional vs. rational)	
Emerging options	

Write a pre-case discussion decision paper. Include these points:

a. options for case resolution
b. criteria (a rational decision should always be made with a set of criteria)
c. analysis of options
d. recommendation (of the best choice among the options)
e. action plan

II. Case Discussion Questions

Big-Picture Analysis

Describe the context of the case.

- ELL Instructional Model
- ELL population

Stakeholders

In small groups, assume the role of one of the case stakeholders. Write a statement/dialogue expressing this person's or group's hypothetical feelings and perspectives. Be prepared to act out your roles to the large group.

- Mr. Richard
- Ann
- Christina
- Rodrigo

Surface Issues

What are the surface issues in this case? What is happening here from an untrained perspective? What underlying assumptions or beliefs feed into this perspective?

Deep Issues

Discuss the real issues in the case. Try to categorize them in terms of language teaching curriculum and instruction.

Evidence-Based Solutions

In groups, develop evidence-based solutions for each deep issue listed. Whenever possible, refer to a theory or principle of language learning and teaching to support your proposed solutions.

Teacher Thinking

In what ways does this case influence and/or reinforce your beliefs and dispositions as a teacher? Consult the Further Readings and Resources section to help with theoretically informed solutions.

III. Post-Case Problem Sets

Post-Case Analysis

A. Categorize what you learned as:
   - teacher knowledge and praxis (e.g., content knowledge, curricular knowledge, pedagogical content knowledge and application)
   - teacher thinking (e.g., beliefs, problem-solving strategies, prioritizing objectives, values, professional ethics, attitudes)

B. List:
   - learning objectives that you discovered in the case
   - potential learning outcomes
   - implications for your pedagogical practices

C. The post-case problem sets introduce reactions from various perspectives. These quotes are from others who have read the cases for educational and pedagogical purposes. Read all of the quotes and then choose two quotes about which to write a short response (put the quotes at the top of each response). Use these questions as a guide:
   - What is the message the speaker is trying to convey? If possible, also explain why you chose the quote.
   - What examples can you think of that connect to the themes presented?
   - Can you relate the quote to a class discussion or to something you have read or experienced?

Quotes

1. "Rodrigo clearly has attention issues, and it is clear the knowledge and experience of his teacher is not being respected by the outside consultant. This is sad and could delay that much needed support he should receive."
2. "The overrepresentation of English learners in special education in the school is alarming and should suggest to the leadership that there is a need for systemic change and professional development provided for teachers on strategies for supporting English learners."
3. "First of all, the novel the students are expected to read during independent reading is far beyond the student's English language proficiency level and requires a great deal of background knowledge. The independent reading time needs to be better tailored and the text adapted to the learner's needs."

D. Write a reflection describing a take-away from the case in terms of praxis. Make sure to develop an action plan to resolve the case. Consider these questions as guidelines:

- In what ways did the case discussion influence your thinking about the case?
- Did you change your original decision or did the discussion reaffirm your position?
- What points had you not considered prior to the case discussion?
- How might the information you gained from this case be applicable to your current instructional setting and/or future instructional settings?
- What did you learn?
- What are you inspired to learn more about?
- How did the themes discussed in class apply to your experience?

E. Discuss what theoretical basis there is for:

- the stakeholders' behaviors in the case.
- the solutions you proposed.

Further Reading and Resources

Brown, J. E., & Doolittle, J. (2008). *A cultural, linguistic, and ecological framework for response to intervention with English language learners.* Tempe, AZ: National Center for Culturally Responsive Educational Systems.

Hamayan, E., Marler, B., Sanchez Lopez, C., & Damico, J. (2007). *Special education considerations for English language learners: Delivering a continuum of services.* Philadelphia: Caslon.

Haynes, J., & Zacarian, D. (2010). *Teaching English language learners across the content areas.* Alexandria, VA: ASCD.

Hoover, J., Klingner, J., Baca, L., & Patton, J. (2007). *Methods for teaching culturally and linguistically diverse exceptional learners.* New York: Merrill/Prentice Hall.

Klingner, J. K., & Edwards, P. A. (2006). Cultural considerations with response to intervention models. *Reading Research Quarterly, 41*(1), 108–117.

Klingner, J. K., & Eppolito, A. (2014). *English language learners: Differentiating between language acquisition and learning disability.* Arlington, VA: Council Exceptional Children (CEC).

Sánchez, M.T., Parker, C., Akbayin, B., & McTigue, A. (2010). *Processes and challenges in identifying learning disabilities among students who are English language learners in three New York State districts.* Issues & Answers Report, REL2010–No. 085. Washington, DC: U.S. Department of Education. http://ies.ed.gov/ncee/edlabs/regions/northeast/pdf/REL_2010085.pdf

Scott, A., Hauerwas, L., & Brown, R. (2013). State policy and guidance for identifying learning disabilities in culturally and linguistically diverse students. *Learning Disability Quarterly, 37*(3), 172–185.

4

Cases in Inclusive World Language Education

The cases in this chapter cover challenging themes that confront world language educators. The *Timberland High* case documents the obstacles a heritage language learner encounters in a Spanish speaking lesson when his teacher does not accept his spoken variety of Spanish as evidenced by her microaggressions masked as error correction. The teacher in the *Whittier Mountain High School* case, Mrs. Anderson, thinks she is using UDL by incorporating an authentic French news channel into her lesson. However, a closer look at the curriculum reveals that she is doing little to support the learning needs of a student with ADHD and an anxiety disorder. In the *Adelesa High School* case, the reader is introduced to a school culture that is convinced that students with learning disabilities should be able to opt out of foreign language instruction. At this same high school, the traditional assessment choices used by a Spanish teacher who teaches a learner with dyslexia prove to be ineffective and she is introduced to alternative forms of assessment for students with learning disabilities.

This chapter encourages critical reflection and dialogue on a range of current and enduring issues in the field of secondary World Language education such as:

- incorporating UDL
- adding in curricular and instructional connections for heritage language learners
- building prior knowledge and previewing vocabulary
- increasing awareness about issues of language, power, and identity

- scaffolding lessons for learners with disabilities
- effectively using authentic materials
- adopting effective approaches to error correction
- avoiding microaggressions and stereotyping
- using differentiated assessments for students with disabilities such as dyslexia, ADHD, and anxiety and for all learners
- incorporating research-based strategies for promoting oral language development

CASE 4.1

Timberland High

Timberland High School serves 1,398 students in Grades 9–12. Minority enrollment is 5 percent of the student body, lower than the state average of 33 percent. The majority of Timberland High students are from affluent homes; they drive their own luxury cars to school and enjoy the privilege of summertime country clubs. Across the train tracks on the south side of town, it looks very different: apartment buildings surround a former mill factory. Within this small section of Timberland, businesses, restaurants, barber shops, community organizations, and bakeries exist where you can hear Spanish, Portuguese, and Cape Verdean Creole. This side of town is home to the majority of the Latinx, Portuguese, and Cape Verdean immigrant and first-generation students who attend Timberland High.

An undercurrent of anti-immigrant sentiment and racial tensions can be felt within this community and is reflected at Timberland High. The majority of students from the south side of town do not take more than the required two years of foreign language, if any. Those who are deemed English learners (ELs) generally take ESL classes in lieu of foreign language so that they can accelerate their mastery of academic English. Minority students in advanced foreign language classes are underrepresented.

Last year, the school received negative press on the state news channels for incidents of racism. When Timberland's local volleyball team played a home game against another state team comprised mostly of Latinx and Black tudents, the Timberland students in the crowd wore American flag shirts and hats and held signs that said, "Go back home." The anti-immigrant and minority rhetoric can be sensed through the existence of Confederate flags signs that say, "English only."

Mario, a Dominican immigrant learner whose family moved to the United States three years ago, was the only Latinx student in his Spanish 1 class. The other bilingual student in the class, Ana Maria, was a short-term exchange student from Madrid, Spain, and also the teacher's pet. During class activities and oral tasks, Mario would tend to omit certain syllables and letters in Spanish. This frustrated Jenny, his teacher, and she would correct his "errors" in front of the class. For example, during a lesson about greetings, instead of saying "*¿Cómo tú estás?*" (how are you?), Mario would say, "*¿Cómo tú ta?*" No matter how many times Jenny tried to rephrase, recast, and directly correct Mario's inaccuracies, he never seemed to get it.

Although people speak Spanish in different ways worldwide and Mario's accent and dialect is quite typical of students coming from the Dominican Republic, Puerto Rico, Cuba, and coastal parts of Colombia, Jenny demonstrated a total lack of appreciation for his home language background. Whenever Mario spoke up in class, the teacher and exchange student from Madrid visibly cringed. Mario noticed this and began to feel ashamed. Mario's spoken Spanish accent and home vocabulary were also reflected in his writing, where he integrated his background knowledge of Spanish. For example, in one written response to a question that asked students to use adjectives and *I* statements, Mario wrote, *Él tá quillao conmigo porque no le presté el dinero* (He was mad because I didn't lend him the money). Even though the linguistic complexity of this response was above and beyond a Level 1 Spanish class, Jenny still chastised Mario for his choice of the informal Dominican "slang" word for *mad*, instead of the "proper" word, *enojado*. Mario always received negative feedback on his vocabulary and pronunciation and was never praised for his linguistic complexity or acknowledged as a language expert in the classroom.

One day, Jenny reached a tipping point. After a long day of teaching, she grew tired of Mario's repetitive errors and resistance to her direct instruction. In an outright disapproval, Jenny told Mario in front of the class, "You need to pronounce your word endings if you **ever** want to speak proper Spanish." Offended, Mario spoke up and said, "Maestra, this is my Dominican accent and you are not going to be able to get rid of it. We do it because it makes our words and sentences flow smoother and faster, not because we are lazy or speak bad Spanish." After having spent two years studying formal Spanish abroad at a university in Madrid, Jenny was certain that the dialect that Mario spoke was miserably incorrect, even inferior in status. Ana Maria, the exchange student from Spain, told Mario, "This kind of pronunciation sounds cheap." Mario could not bear the shame of having to defend his identity and stormed out of class. Found in the hallway, a teacher sent him to the vice principal's office where Mario explained the poor treatment he had received.

Because of the negative press Timberland High had received earlier and a new schoolwide focus on equity training, the vice principal asked the chair of the World Language Department to "have a talk" with Jenny and see how she could support her and this student. Mario had decided to mentally check out of the class and only speak when called upon. Frustrated, Jenny brought this to the attention of her department chair, Lynn, who recently attended a mandatory workshop about educational equity. "I don't know why Mario has become so passive and defiant in my class. He chooses not to engage and participate just because I brought to his attention the errors he was making in his Spanish. He cannot go around saying and writing *pa* instead of *para* or *na* instead of *nada*," explained Jenny. Lynn advised Jenny, "Make sure your curriculum includes culture goals. Look at the C in the ACTFL guidelines (https://www.actfl.org/resources/world-readiness-standards-learning-languages/standards-summary) and make sure you include some cultural understandings. This will allow us to share what we did to manage the equity issue here. This is culturally responsive teaching."

Two weeks later, Jenny was happy to report that she meticulously included culture in her classroom and provided Lynn with her syllabus (see Exhibit A).

Exhibit A: Curricular Plan and Objectives

Chapter 2: Nice to Meet You: Location: Madrid, Spain

Language Goals

Students will:

- say *hello* and *goodbye*.
- introduce people and respond to an introduction.
- ask how someone is and say how he/she is.
- ask and say how old someone is.
- ask where someone is from and say where he/she is from.
- talk about likes and dislikes.
- tell what is in their room.

Cultural Understandings

Students will:

- give details about the extended family.
- describe their school uniform.
- discuss an apartment in Spain/sharing a TV set.
- identify greetings

Chapter 3: New Classes and New Friends: Location: Madrid, Spain

Language Goals

Students will:

- talk about classes and sequencing events.
- discuss the time of day.
- tell at what time something happens.
- talk about being late or in a hurry.
- describe people and things.
- talk about things they like and explain why.

Cultural Understandings

Students will:

- compare the class schedule in Spain and the U.S.
- compare the grading system in Spain and the U.S.
- discuss the custom of the *siesta* in Spain.
- use titles of respect appropriately.
- compare a typical school day in Spain and the U.S.

I. Pre-Case Discussion Problem Sets

Complete the chart after reading the case.

Facts	
Opinions	
Assumptions	
Theories referred or connected to (if any)	
Ambiguous language	
Criteria you used in analyzing the case (e.g., emotional vs. rational)	
Emerging options	

Write a pre-case discussion decision paper. Include these points:

a. options for case resolution
b. criteria (a rational decision should always be made with a set of criteria)
c. analysis of options
d. recommendation (of the best choice among the options)
e. action plan

II. Case Discussion Questions

Big-Picture Analysis

Describe the context of the case.

- Timberland High student demographics
- Community and school context
- World Language curriculum

Stakeholders

In small groups, assume the role of one of the case stakeholders. Write a statement/ dialogue expressing this person's or group's hypothetical feelings and perspectives. Be prepared to act out your roles to the large group.

- Mario
- Jenny
- Lynn
- Other students in the classroom

Surface Issues

What are the surface issues in this case? What is happening here from an untrained perspective? What underlying assumptions or beliefs feed into this perspective?

Deep Issues

Discuss the real issues in the case. Try to categorize them in terms of language teaching curriculum and instruction.

Evidence-Based Solutions

In groups, develop evidence-based solutions for each deep issue listed. Whenever possible, refer to a theory or principle of language learning and teaching to support your proposed solutions.

Teacher Thinking

In what ways does this case influence and/or reinforce your beliefs and dispositions as a teacher? Consult the Further Readings and Resources section to help with theoretically informed solutions.

III. Post-Case Problem Sets

Post-Case Analysis

A. Categorize what you learned as:
  - teacher knowledge and praxis (e.g., content knowledge, curricular knowledge, pedagogical content knowledge and application)
  - teacher thinking (e.g., beliefs, problem-solving strategies, prioritizing objectives, values, professional ethics, attitudes)

B. List:
  - learning objectives that you discovered in the case
  - potential learning outcomes
  - implications for your pedagogical practices

C. The post-case problem sets introduce reactions from various perspectives. These quotes are from others who have read the cases for educational and pedagogical purposes. Read all of the quotes and then choose two quotes about which to write a short response (put the quotes at the top of each response). Use these questions as a guide:
  - What is the message the speaker is trying to convey? If possible, also explain why you chose the quote.
  - What examples can you think of that connect to the themes presented?
  - Can you relate the quote to a class discussion or to something you have read or experienced?

Quotes

1. "Mario really probably belongs in an ESL class instead of Spanish, especially since he probably already knows the language and needs to polish his English."
2. "The teacher should be fired immediately. This type of linguistic and cultural racism cannot be supported and should not be disguised as a form of error correction."
3. "To promote all learners' academic spoken Spanish, the teacher could have provided sentence starters or a vocabulary word bank. Overall, she needs to create a supportive and safe atmosphere for all learners to be able to take risks with the language."

D. Write a reflection describing a take-away from the case in terms of praxis. Make sure to develop an action plan to resolve the case. Consider these questions as guidelines:
- In what ways did the case discussion influence your thinking about the case?
- Did you change your original decision or did the discussion reaffirm your position?
- What points had you not considered prior to the case discussion?
- How might the information you gained from this case be applicable to your current instructional setting and/or future instructional settings?
- What did you learn?
- What are you inspired to learn more about?
- How did the themes discussed in class apply to your experience?

E. Discuss what theoretical basis there is for:
- the stakeholders' behaviors in the case.
- the solutions you proposed.

Further Reading and Resources

American Academy of Arts and Sciences. (2017). *America's languages: Investing in language education for the 21st century*. Cambridge, MA: American Academy of Arts and Sciences. https://www.amacad.org/publication/americas-languages

Brecht, R. D., & Ingold, C. W. (2002). *Tapping a national resource: Heritage languages in the United States*. Report ED464515. Washington, DC: ERIC Publications.

Carreira, M. (2007). Spanish for native speakers matters: Narrowing the Latino academic gap through Spanish language instruction. *Heritage Language Journal*, *5*(1), 147–171. Retrieved from www.heritagelanguages.org

Fairclough, M., Beudrie, S., Valdes, G., & Roca, A. (2016). *Innovative strategies for heritage language teaching: A practical guide for the classroom*. Washington, DC: Georgetown University Press.

Hendrickson, J. (1978). Error correction in foreign language teaching: Recent theory, research, and practice. *Modern Language Journal, 62*, 387–398.

Kubota, R., & Lin, A. (2009). *Race, class, identity in second language education: Exploring critically engaged practice*. New York: Routledge.

Paris, D., & Alim, H. S. (2014). What are we seeking to sustain through culturally sustaining pedagogy? A loving critique forward. *Harvard Educational Review*, *84*(1), 85–100.

Roca, A., Colombi, C., & Valdez, G. (2000). *Mi lengua: Spanish as a heritage language in the United States: Research and practice*. Washington, DC: Georgetown University Press.

Webb, J., & Miller, B. (2000). *Teaching heritage language learners: Voices from the classroom*. Alexandria, VA: American Council on the Teaching of Foreign Languages.

CASE 4.2
Whittier Mountain High School

Standing impatiently at the threshold of the World Language Director's office at Whitter Mountain High School, Mrs. Anderson felt the time eased by the beautiful snowfall through the sunlit forest that served as a truly breathtaking backdrop to learning and teaching. To her left, Mrs. Anderson saw a welcome board displayed for parents and visitors that included the following school mission:

The Whittier Mountain School District will take a leading role advocating a progressive and inclusive education for all learners in our schools. The mission of Whittier Mountain High is to educate every learner through a comprehensive and rigorous curriculum taught in a safe, nurturing, and inclusive environment. We encourage students to pursue their dreams, succeed with excellence, integrity, and contribute meaningfully to a diverse society.

In her eagerness to incorporate new strategies in her class, Mrs. Anderson, a French teacher at Whittier Mountain High School, integrated an authentic French news channel into her curriculum so that she could develop students' listening comprehension skills. Typically, Mrs. Bisset, the director of the World Language Department, conducts bi-annual observations with follow-up meetings for each of the three teachers in her department. Following her observation of Mrs. Anderson's lesson, Mrs. Bisset requested an emergency meeting to express her concerns when observing this lesson. As Mrs. Anderson waited outside the director's office as Mrs. Bisset finished a phone call, Mrs. Anderson thought back to her curricular decisions.

Mrs. Anderson decided to incorporate France Television into her unit on issues in modern-day France because it is France's national TV broadcasting company. She thought that there would be no better way to understand modern-day topics and challenges in France than to have her students watch the news. She was proud of how she was growing in her professional practice. Over the summer, after having attended a local foreign language education conference and a districtwide professional development training, she was persuaded to integrate more authentic learning and UDL into her teaching. As such, she thought an authentic news interview would be a multi-modal form of representation that would be authentic and meaningful to her French 2 students, most of whom were in tenth grade.

During the lesson that Mrs. Bisset observed, Mrs. Anderson had 26 students sitting in rows in her classroom. Since this French 2 class was right after lunch, students walked in talking loudly. Mrs. Anderson tried unsuccessfully to get their attention until one of her students told his peers to "chill." Mrs. Anderson jumped right into the lesson, without any framing or explanation of objectives. "Ok, we are going to watch a video today," Mrs. Anderson said. "I want you to take notes. No goofing around."

The news excerpt Mrs. Anderson selected, translated into English, was titled, "What Challenges Will French Businesses Face and How Strong Is France's Economy in the 21st Century?" She played the video, which featured a reporter interviewing an economics professor from a well-known French university. This an excerpt from the French news video, translated here into English; when played for the students, the excerpt displayed no captions in English or French and Mrs. Anderson did not provide any background discussion or readings before the lesson to frame the content:

> Economists in France are concerned about the optimal distribution of scare resources within French society. For example, they are pondering over what modern-day French consumers like and how firms produce goods and which goods people buy. As an economist, I am also thinking deeply about how, if, and whether the government should intervene in the economy to strengthen societal economic welfare. The whole society is impacted by issues such as economic growth and unemployment.

For the rest of the interview, which lasted 28 minutes, the economics professor offered his perspective on the overall strengths and challenges of France's modern economy and involved high-level technical vocabulary specific to the field of economics, such as *macroeconomics, consumer behavior,* and *economic systems.*

Mrs. Bisset noticed that half the class failed to take notes. She was particularly concerned that Rose, a student with an individualized education plan, was not receiving the supports she needed to access the lesson. "I think there were missed opportunities to engage and support learners in this lesson," she told Mrs. Anderson, during their follow-up meeting. In her defense of the lesson design, Mrs. Anderson said, "The website encompasses six different channels, each of which has a distinct editorial strategy and reporting style. Needless to say, tuning into French TV is a highly effective way to bring your students closer to the French culture! This is what I have done. It is called authentic learning. In addition, my lesson offered a multimodal representation of content, which should, according to UDL, actively engage my students. This is just unacceptable behavior and inattention on behalf of the students."

Rose, a student in Mrs. Anderson's French 2 class, has ADHD and an anxiety disorder. Exhibit A contains some of the accommodations included in her individualized education plan. At Whittier Mountain High, all tenth grade–content area teachers are expected to implement these supports for Rose into their lessons. However, because of the misconception among faculty about the status of world language classes as non-core subjects, the "core" content-area teachers for math, science, and social studies often meet about students without inviting or communicating decisions with "extracurricular" classes.

Throughout the video, Mrs. Anderson noticed that Rose was "goofing off" and talking with her peers in the back of the room. She redirected her attention when given a warning from the teacher. At the end of the video, Mrs. Anderson asked the students to write their responses to listening comprehension questions (see Exhibit B). While everyone else was working independently and quietly, Rose was busy doodling pictures and telling jokes with friends. She barely wrote a complete sentence. She wasn't the only one; many students left more than three questions blank. However, Mrs. Anderson zeroed in on the disruptive and rude behavior of Rose.

Exhibit A: Individualized Learning Plan for Rose

- Give directions out loud and in writing and have the student repeat them.
- Provide a lesson outline that details instructions and assignments.
- Keep instructions clear, simple, and accurate.
- Set up preferential seating close to the teacher.
- Break down assignments into smaller chunks.
- Check in frequently for understanding and "emotional temperature."
- Provide a signal before calling on the student and a signal for the student to opt out of answering.

Exhibit B: Listening Comprehension Questions for France TV Economist Interview

1. What did the French economist say about the economic resilience and growth of France despite the global slowdown?
2. How are France's fiscal policies connected to rising debt and spending trends?
3. How would you describe the economic outlook for France? Use data from the interview.
4. In what ways is sustained unemployment a drag on social security nets in France?
5. According to the professor, what is the solution to France's sluggish competitiveness?

I. Pre-Case Discussion Problem Sets

Complete the chart after reading the case.

Facts	
Opinions	
Assumptions	
Theories referred or connected to (if any)	
Ambiguous language	
Criteria you used in analyzing the case (e.g., emotional vs. rational)	
Emerging options	

Write a pre-case discussion decision paper. Include these points:

a. options for case resolution
b. criteria (a rational decision should always be made with a set of criteria)
c. analysis of options
d. recommendation (of the best choice among the options)
e. action plan

II. Case Discussion Questions

Big-Picture Analysis

Describe the context of the case.

- School policy for students with disabilities and world languages
- Educator and family perceptions of world language classes
- School inclusive excellence vision and teacher instructional approaches

Stakeholders

In small groups, assume the role of one of the case stakeholders. Write a statement/ dialogue expressing this person's or group's hypothetical feelings and perspectives. Be prepared to act out your roles to the large group.

- Mrs. Anderson
- Rose
- Mrs. Bisset
- Other learners

Surface Issues

What are the surface issues in this case? What is happening here from an untrained perspective? What underlying assumptions or beliefs feed into this perspective?

Deep Issues

Discuss the real issues are in the case. Try to categorize them in terms of language teaching curriculum and instruction.

Evidence-Based Solutions

In groups, develop evidence-based solutions for each deep issue listed. Whenever possible, refer to a theory or principle of language learning and teaching to support your proposed solutions.

Teacher Thinking

In what ways does this case influence and/or reinforce your beliefs and dispositions as a teacher? Consult the Further Readings and Resources section to help with theoretically informed solutions.

III. Post-Case Problem Sets

Post-Case Analysis

A. Categorize what you learned as:
   - teacher knowledge and praxis (e.g., content knowledge, curricular knowledge, pedagogical content knowledge and application)
   - teacher thinking (e.g., beliefs, problem-solving strategies, prioritizing objectives, values, professional ethics, attitudes)

B. List:
   - learning objectives that you discovered in the case
   - potential learning outcomes
   - implications for your pedagogical practices

C. The post-case problem sets introduce reactions from various perspectives. These quotes are from others who have read the cases for educational and pedagogical purposes. Read all of the quotes and then choose two quotes about which to write a short response (put the quotes at the top of each response). Use these questions as a guide:
   - What is the message the speaker is trying to convey? If possible, also explain why you chose the quote.
   - What examples can you think of that connect to the themes presented?
   - Can you relate the quote to a class discussion or to something you have read or experienced?

Quotes

1. "Mrs. Anderson has the right pedagogical ideas with the wrong instructional and curricular applications. She needs to be more receptive to feedback."
2. "Authentic materials are a great way to engage learners but you need to build background knowledge, pre-teach hard vocabulary, and pause frequently. Not to mention, the topic of the lesson was dry and meaningless to young learners."
3. "She is using UDL and authentic materials in the lesson—the director of World Language should keep out of it and let her grow. Rose will be able to follow along with the summaries of other learners if she didn't catch the gist of the video."

D. Write a reflection describing a take-away from the case in terms of praxis. Make sure to develop an action plan to resolve the case. Consider these questions as guidelines:
   - In what ways did the case discussion influence your thinking about the case?
   - Did you change your original decision or did the discussion reaffirm your position?
   - What points had you not considered prior to the case discussion?
   - How might the information you gained from this case be applicable to your current instructional setting and/or future instructional settings?
   - What did you learn?
   - What are you inspired to learn more about?
   - How did the themes discussed in class apply to your experience?

E. Discuss what theoretical basis there is for:
   - the stakeholders' behaviors in the case.
   - the solutions you proposed.

Further Reading and Resources

Abrams, Z. (2008). Alternative second language curricula for learners with disabilities: Two case studies. *Modern Language Journal, 92*(3), 414–430.

Banks, T. (2008). Foreign language learning difficulties and teaching strategies. Online Submission. Washington, DC: ERIC.

Brualdi, A.C. (1996). *Multiple intelligences: Gardner's theory*. Washington, DC: ERIC Clearinghouse on Assessment and Evaluation, ED410226 1996-09-00.

Duval, E. (2006). Including students with learning disabilities in the foreign language class. *Journal of Teaching Exceptional Children, 38*(6).

Leons, E., Herbert, C., & Gobbo, K. (2009). Students with learning disabilities and AD/HD in the foreign language classroom: Supporting students and instructors. *Foreign Language Annals, 42*(1), 42–54.

Lerner, J. W. (1991). Critical issues in learning disabilities: Foreign language learning. *Learning Disabilities Research and Practice, 6*(1), 50–53.

McColl, H. (2005). Foreign language learning and inclusion: Who? why? what?—and how? *Support for Learning, 20*(3), 103–108.

Polio, C., & Zyzik, E. (2017). *Authentic materials myths: Applying second language research to classroom teaching*. Ann Arbor: University of Michigan Press.

Sparks, R., Javorsky, J., & Philips, L. (2005). Comparison of the performance of college students classified as ADHD, LD, and LD/ADHD in foreign language courses. *Language Learning, 55*(1), 151–177.

CASE 4.3

Adelesa High School

According to Adelesa High School's website, "world language instruction is an important part of Adelesa School District's efforts to provide challenging educational programs in its public school and to prepare students to compete in a global world. Knowledge and skills that students acquire in foreign language classes reinforce and expand learning in other subject areas."

At the secondary level, the World Language Standards of Learning set learning targets and expectations for what students should know and be able to do by the end of each course offered for a standard unit of credit.

Under current graduation requirements, courses in a world language are optional for students seeking a standard diploma. However, it is a requirement for students seeking an advanced studies diploma. Most students seeking college admission are strongly advised to receive an advanced studies diploma. Just over 12 percent of students with disabilities are meeting the requirements for the desired advanced studies diploma. It is thought that one of the factors contributing to this level of obtainment may be the world language requirement.

Many of the parents and teachers of Adelesa feel that students with learning disabilities should not be required to take a world language. During the last academic year, the new superintendent wanted to require **all** learners to take a world language, which teachers and parents pushed back against. Ultimately, the optional world language track remained intact for the standard diploma and only students with disabilities opting for a world language class as part of the advanced diploma requirement would take it.

Consequently, World Language teachers in the district have not been prepared to understand—let alone respond to—the needs of students with various disabilities in their classes. There is no professional development in this area and none of the six World Language teachers in the school have received any formal training on strategies for making foreign language accessible to students with disabilities. Many learning disabilities have an influence on how language is perceived, processed, and expressed, but the large majority of teacher preparation programs for world language education in the area do not provide courses on how to meaningfully support these students in the classroom and promote language learning.

Mrs. Martinez is the tenth grade Spanish teacher at Adelesa High School. Originally from Spain, she received her MA in Hispanic Language and Literature and has been teaching high school Spanish for more than 10 years. She is an energetic and passionate teacher who loves her subject matter, but she sticks to the script and follows the traditional textbook. She provides no supplementary instructional materials or classroom-based assessments. Moreover, without realizing it, she shows subtle preference or bias when calling on students in the classroom to respond to her questions. She tends to call on the more advanced speakers. Her goal is to get through as much of the textbook as possible for the school year; she feels the pressure to prepare students with "serious foreign language aims for junior and senior year." She feels that students with disabilities slow down the pace of her course. In a discussion with Maureen, a colleague in her department, Mrs. Martinez noted, "I don't know how to help Jillian, a student with dyslexia in my Spanish 2 class. I just do not have the time to provide her with the one-on-one support she would need to succeed in foreign language learning. She leaves her daily written assessments and quizzes incomplete, but she is active in class discussions. I know she is learning, so why is she failing the assessments? It is such a burden for me to figure this all out." Exhibit A includes the latest exit slip, or daily formative assessment of preterite and perfect tenses in her class.

Maureen tried to explain to Mrs. Martinez that she was using traditional assessments and teaching techniques that, although taken from the textbook, do not allow students with learning disabilities to express and access their learning. She said, "Although your book-based tests are scored easily and quickly because items are often multiple choice, matching, fill in the blank, or true/false, they may not be the best way for students like Jillian to express what they know. Have you ever considered the use of portfolios, journals, or performance-based activities as alternative assessments? Do you provide rubrics?"

Mrs. Martinez responded, "I wouldn't even begin to know how to fairly grade students using portfolios. I think it is a good idea in theory, but not in practice. It requires a lot of planning and creativity, not to mention the equity issues. I mean, how can I actually fairly grade students who work harder than others? I use ongoing daily assessments in the form of quizzes in my Spanish class, so at least I am using formative and summative assessments. I mean, they cannot expect me to change my whole teaching for one student."

Exhibit A: Exit Slip Formative Daily Assessment of Grammar

Direcciones (Directions)

A. Rellena la able con las formas conjugadas de los verbos (Complete the graph with the form of the correctly conjugated verbs):

	yo (I)	tú (you)	él (he)	nosotros (we)	vosotros (you, plural, spain)
ser (to be)					
trabajar (to work)					
ir (to go)					
ver (to see)					
beber (to drink)					

B. Completa la actividad con las formas del Pretérito Imperfecto. (Complete the activity with forms of imperfect preterite.)

1, Mi tío (ser) __________ una persona muy seria. (My uncle was a very serious person.)

2, Con mis amigos (ir, nosotros) __________ al cine (With my friends, we all were going to the movie.)

3, Siempre (hablar, él) __________ de política y religión. (He always talked about politics and religion.)

4, Nuestra casa (estar) __________ al lado del mercado donde (haber) __________ mucha gente. (Our house was located on the side of the market where there were many people.)

5, Ahora no fumo pero antes (fumar, yo) __________ mucho. (Now I don't smoke, but before I smoked a lot.)

6, Mientras (comer, ellos) __________ (mirar, ellos) __________ la tele. (While they were eating, they were watching the television.)

7, (Ser) __________ un día frío de invierno. Las estrellas (brillar) __________ en el cielo. (It was a cold winter day. The stars were shining in the sky.)

8, (Ir, vosotros) __________ a la escuela de lunes a viernes. (You all were going to the school from Monday to Wednesday.)

C. ¿Puedes elegir cuál forma es el pretérito imperfecto? (Can you choose which form is imperfect preterite?)

viví, trabajaba, era, preguntaste, veo, hablando, trabaja, trabajaré, comí, comíamos, poniendo, ponía, pongo, puse, llamaba, estudio, escribía, veía, ví, roto, conquistaba

I. Pre-Case Discussion Problem Sets

Complete the chart after reading the case.

Facts	
Opinions	
Assumptions	
Theories referred or connected to (if any)	
Ambiguous language	
Criteria you used in analyzing the case (e.g., emotional vs. rational)	
Emerging options	

Write a pre-case discussion decision paper. Include these points:

a. options for case resolution
b. criteria (a rational decision should always be made with a set of criteria)
c. analysis of options
d. recommendation (of the best choice among the options)
e. action plan

II. Case Discussion Questions

Big-Picture Analysis

Describe the context of the case.

- student demographics
- school district
- community perspectives on foreign language learning

Stakeholders

In small groups, assume the role of one of the case stakeholders. Write a statement/dialogue expressing this person's or group's hypothetical feelings and perspectives. Be prepared to act out your roles to the large group.

- Mrs. Martinez
- Jillian
- Maureen

Surface Issues

What are the surface issues in this case? What is happening here from an untrained perspective? What underlying assumptions or beliefs feed into this perspective?

Deep Issues

Discuss the real issues in the case. Try to categorize them in terms of language teaching curriculum and instruction.

Evidence-Based Solutions

In groups, develop evidence-based solutions for each deep issue listed. Whenever possible, refer to a theory or principle of language learning and teaching to support your proposed solutions.

Teacher Thinking

In what ways does this case influence and/or reinforce your beliefs and dispositions as a teacher? Consult the Further Readings and Resources section to help with theoretically informed solutions.

III. Post-Case Problem Sets

Post-Case Analysis

A. Categorize what you learned as:
   - teacher knowledge and praxis (e.g., content knowledge, curricular knowledge, pedagogical content knowledge and application)
   - teacher thinking (e.g., beliefs, problem-solving strategies, prioritizing objectives, values, professional ethics, attitudes)

B. List:
   - learning objectives that you discovered in the case
   - potential learning outcomes
   - implications for your pedagogical implications

C. The post-case problem sets introduce reactions from various perspectives. These quotes are from others who have read the cases for educational and pedagogical purposes. Read all of the quotes and then choose two quotes about which to write a short response (put the quotes at the top of each response). Use these questions as a guide:
   - What is the message the speaker is trying to convey? If possible, also explain why you chose the quote.
   - What examples can you think of that connect to the themes presented?
   - Can you relate the quote to a class discussion or to something you have read or experienced?

Quotes

1. "Mrs. Martinez doesn't realize that her assessments are totally inaccessible to students with dyslexia and other learning disabilities. She should incorporate more hands-on and real-life informal assessments with rubrics."
2. "The burden always falls on teachers to support students with limited resources and training. Mrs. Martinez should only have to teach students who are capable of learning foreign languages."
3. "The school should abolish the two diploma tracks altogether as the structure alone promotes segregation."

D. Write a reflection describing a take-away from the case in terms of praxis. Make sure to develop an action plan to resolve the case. Consider these questions as guidelines:

- In what ways did the case discussion influence your thinking about the case?
- Did you change your original decision or did the discussion reaffirm your position?
- What points had you not considered prior to the case discussion?
- How might the information you gained from this case be applicable to your current instructional setting and/or future instructional settings?
- What did you learn?
- What are you inspired to learn more about?
- How did the themes discussed in class apply to your experience?

E. Discuss what theoretical basis there is for:

- the stakeholders' behaviors in the case.
- the solutions you proposed.

Further Reading and Resources

Blaz, D. (2006). *Differentiated instruction: A guide for foreign language teachers.* New York: Routledge.

Blaz, D. (2013). *A collection of performance tasks and rubric in foreign language.* New York: Routledge.

Ganschow, L., & Sparks, R. (2001). Learning difficulties and foreign language learning: A review of research and instruction. *Language Teaching, 34,* 79–98.

Omaggio Hadley, A. (2001). *Teaching language in context* (3rd ed.). Boston: Thomson Heinle.

Schneider, E., & Crombie, M. (2003). *Dyslexia and foreign language learning.* London: Fulton Publishers.

Scott, S., & Edwards, W. (2012). *Disability and world language learning: Inclusive teaching for diverse learners.* New York: Rowman & Littlefield.

5

Cases in Inclusive Post-Secondary English for Academic Purposes

The cases in this chapter deal with the complexities of the EAP classroom at the post-secondary level. The first case, *Northwood University*, highlights the importance of including international, nonnative English–speaking undergraduate students into college courses; specific focus areas in this case include cultural considerations and thoughtful grouping for project-based learning. *Fort Crimson*, the second case, discusses how to support the writing development of a learner who is visually impaired via inclusive techniques and facilitate her social inclusion in the College ESL Writing course. The final case, *Shoreham English Language Institute*, presents the challenges of promoting oral language, reading-to-speaking connections, and higher-order thinking in a diverse group of students with a range of backgrounds and linguistic proficiencies and highlights the importance of ground rules for respectful and inclusive academic conversations. The chapter discusses inclusive language teaching and learning concepts such as:

- effectively planning project-based learning and thoughtful grouping
- promoting inclusive and differentiated teaching and learning for culturally and linguistically diverse learners in higher education and EAP settings

- assessing learners' prior knowledge and experiences and tailoring curriculum to match their strengths and areas of need
- supporting educational access and inclusion of students with physical disabilities in EAP via research-based scaffolds
- applying UDL principles in second language teaching and learning in higher education
- establishing reading-to-writing connections to promote higher-order thinking
- establishing ground rules and infusing sentence starters to promote respectful academic conversations about controversial issues

CASE 5.1

Northwood University

Northwood University is a historically white institution; 88 percent of the most recent graduating class was made up of middle-upper class white women and 97 percent of the faculty and upper administration is also white middle-upper class.

"I don't know what to do next," said Mustapha to his academic advisor. "I was a great student back home but here I am struggling. I am surely failing two of my three classes. I don't know if this college right for me. Maybe I should consider transferring to another university, one that is more open to international students."

Dr. Riley, Mustapha's academic advisor, sighed. This was the second such case she had had to deal with this semester—being placed in the uncomfortable position of mentoring a student who feels gravely misunderstood, underestimated, and marginalized. Last semester, she had an advisee named Maria who was a journalist for a national newspaper in Brazil, but here she was told by professors that there were serious issues with the quality of her writing and who questioned her ability to meet her academic requirements. She was put on academic probation, something absolutely stigmatizing in her culture. Devastated by the ongoing negative feedback, low grades, lack of support and empathy, and her inability to express her understanding of key concepts in sophisticated English, she considered dropping out of the program. As an immigrant, Maria made a huge financial sacrifice to attend classes and, ultimately, she decided to drop out of the program altogether. Dr. Riley often wondered what she could have done to prevent Maria from dropping out.

Dr. Riley is a fierce advocate of diversity on campus. She feels it is an asset but knows that many faculty members feel differently. When students feel unwelcome here, it bothers her. To avoid a similar outcome, she asked Mustapha to tell her more. Mustapha relayed the most recent events.

> "For your final assignment, you will work with a group of classmates to identify what you deem to be a pressing social issue of campus. Adopting the principles learned in this course, I ask you to co-author a strategic plan of action for resolving the issue. This assignment is designed to be meaningful and relevant, so please think carefully about a serious issue on campus and develop a solution and plan of action," announced Professor Benson to his undergraduate Project Management course at

Northwood University. Students shuffled around into groups. As usual, Mustapha, the only international student and student of color in the class, looked over to find a semi-friendly face, usually a kind female, to give him a nonverbal cue that her group could use one more person.

It has been difficult for Mustapha to form social relationships with his American classmates. He feels that his ideas are often dismissed in class or that his professors and classmates secretly laugh at his accent or "inarticulate English," as he defines it. Even though he is a respected member of a very successful family back home in Tunisia, he feels that he is not viewed with the same respect or intelligence as he is back in his home country. He lives off campus with a group of international students who attend other local area colleges.

Mustapha finally found a group of students to join. He is not at all accustomed to this style of learning. Back home, students would never work in groups on a final paper. How would the teacher know how much knowledge each student contributed? He felt this assignment was quite odd, but he tried to keep an open mind.

He was in a group with Jenny, Bob, Ashley, and Kim. Ashley and Jenny immediately insisted that rape on campus was the most important issue. Jenny proposed developing a strategic marketing plan of action to raise awareness of this issue. Bob agreed that this would be a good topic; he also thought that the terrible cafeteria food could be another topic. Jenny then suggested that they flip a coin between the two topics. Mustapha, never shy to share his opinion, immediately spoke up and said, "Although your proposals are also serious, they are not as important as the lack of integration of minority student populations, including foreign, immigrant, and Black students. Besides, I don't think the females here will be too comfortable talking about rape in front of the men and we should be respectful of them. Besides, food is just not serious enough." Bob replied, "No, I disagree. I think we will just stick to what is happening to everyone. This is too bad too but speaking about rape or food are topics that affect all students on campus." Jenny concurred, "I totally agree." Bob, Ashley, and Kim all rolled their

> eyes and proceeded to plan a timeline for workload completion on a topic with which Mustapha did not agree. Not to mention, he caught their glances and eye roles and felt misjudged.
>
> Feeling dismissed once more, Mustapha decided to speak to Professor Benson after class about the issue. He told Professor Benson, "I would prefer to choose a topic that is meaningful and relevant, and improving diversity and treatment on campus is very important." Professor Benson asked Mustapha what the students in his group felt about the topic. When Mustapha told them their proposals, Professor Benson replied, "Well, Mustapha, welcome to the democratic process. The majority wins. I am sorry but you will just have to settle on the topic your group has selected." Mustapha did not want to argue with his professor so he accepted his words but felt very upset about having his idea, yet again, dismissed. He did not want to mention how internally upset he felt about researching a topic as sensitive as rape alongside female peers. He did not want to mention that he was worried about his grade depending on successful group work.
>
> Thus far, Professor Benson has assigned Mustapha two Ds and one C- on three of his four course papers. Mustapha is quite concerned about doing well on the final project so that he can improve his grade and bring up his GPA.
>
> He never received such low scores in his home country. His English is intermediate/advanced and he makes frequent grammatical errors in his writing. However, when he looks at his feedback from Professor Benson, all he sees are lots of underlined sentences with the letters "akwd" written above it. When he looks at the grading rubric, he is often given the highest grade for content but the lowest grade for structure and coherence.

After hearing Mustapha's reflection, Dr. Riley knew something had to be done, but she didn't know what. She attended the associate provost's presentation on retention and enrollment issues, and the numbers (see Exhibit A) alarmed her. The university already has little diversity (see Exhibit B). As an employee of the university and an empathetic person, she was conflicted about how to best advise Mustapha. She felt as though she was caught between a rock and a hard place.

Exhibit A: Retention Data

Percentage of Culturally and Linguistically Diverse Students (International and Immigrant Students) Who Drop Out of Programs

- Academic Year 2017: 15 percent
- Academic Year 2018: 16 percent
- Academic Year 2019: 21 percent

Exhibit B: Diversity Dashboard Data of Student Demographics

- 88 percent white
- 8 percent BIPOC
- 2 percent international

I. Pre-Case Discussion Problem Sets

Complete the chart after reading the case.

Facts	
Opinions	
Assumptions	
Theories referred or connected to (if any)	
Ambiguous language	
Criteria you used in analyzing the case (e.g., emotional vs. rational)	
Emerging options	

Write a pre-case discussion decision paper. Include these points:

a. options for case resolution
b. criteria (a rational decision should always be made with a set of criteria)
c. analysis of options
d. recommendation (of the best choice among the options)
e. action plan

II. Case Discussion Questions

Big-Picture Analysis

Describe the context of the case.

- university climate
- classroom context

Stakeholders

In small groups, assume the role of one of the case stakeholders. Write a statement/ dialogue expressing this person's or group's hypothetical feelings and perspectives. Be prepared to act out your roles to the large group.

- Dr. Riley
- Mustapha
- Maria
- Dr. Benson
- Jenny, Bob, Ashley, and Kim

Surface Issues

What are the surface issues in this case? What is happening here from an untrained perspective? What underlying assumptions or beliefs feed into this perspective?

Deep Issues

Discuss the real issues in the case. Try to categorize them in terms of language teaching curriculum and instruction.

Evidence-Based Solutions

In groups, develop evidence-based solutions for each deep issue listed. Whenever possible, refer to a theory or principle of language learning and teaching to support your proposed solutions.

Teacher Thinking

In what ways does this case influence and/or reinforce your beliefs and dispositions as a teacher? Consult the Further Readings and Resources section to help with theoretically informed solutions.

III. Post-Case Problem Sets

Post-Case Analysis

A. Categorize what you learned as:
   - teacher knowledge and praxis (e.g., content knowledge, curricular knowledge, pedagogical content knowledge and application)
   - teacher thinking (e.g., beliefs, problem-solving strategies, prioritizing objectives, values, professional ethics, attitudes)

B. List:
   - learning objectives that you discovered in the case
   - potential learning outcomes
   - implications for your pedagogical practices

C. The post-case problem sets introduce reactions from various perspectives. These quotes are from others who have read the cases for educational and pedagogical purposes. Read all of the quotes and then choose two quotes about which to write a short response (put the quotes at the top of each response). Use these questions as a guide:
   - What is the message the speaker is trying to convey? If possible, also explain why you chose the quote.
   - What examples can you think of that connect to the themes presented?
   - Can you relate the quote to a class discussion or to something you have read or experienced?

Quotes

1. "It would be valuable for the teacher and advisor to gather background information to support these two learners. We forget about the importance of identifying our learner's needs and backgrounds."
2. "Dr. Benson shouldn't have to shift his entire pedagogical style to meet the need of one international student. After all, if these students come here, they should quickly adjust to our expectations."
3. "Clearly, the teacher needs to incorporate flexible grouping and model expectations for effective and equitable collaboration. This embarrassing situation could have been averted with some careful planning or modifications."

D. Write a reflection describing a take-away from the case in terms of praxis. Make sure to develop an action plan to resolve the case. Consider these questions as guidelines:

- In what ways did the case discussion influence your thinking about the case?
- Did you change your original decision or did the discussion reaffirm your position?
- What points had you not considered prior to the case discussion?
- How might the information you gained from this case be applicable to your current instructional setting and/or future instructional settings?
- What did you learn?
- What are you inspired to learn more about?
- How did the themes discussed in class apply to your experience?

E. Discuss what theoretical basis there is for:

- the stakeholders' behaviors in the case.
- the solutions you proposed.

Further Reading and Resources

Carrol, J., & Ryan, J. (2006). *Teaching international students: Improving learning for all.* New York: Routledge.

Gras-Velazquez, A. (2019). *Project-based learning in second language acquisition: Building communities of practice in higher education.* New York: Routledge.

Kimmel, K., & Volet, V. (2012). University students' perceptions of and attitudes towards culturally diverse group work: Does context matter? *Journal of Studies in International Education, 16*(2), 157–181.

Kubota, R., & Lin, A. (2009). *Race, class, identity in second language education: Exploring critically engaged practice.* New York: Routledge.

Moriña, A., Cortés-Vega, M. D., & Molina, V. M. (2015). Faculty training: An unavoidable requirement for approaching more inclusive university classrooms. *Teaching in Higher Education, 20*(8), 795–806.

Nuñez, A. M., & Sparks, P. J. (2012). Who are linguistic minority students in higher education? An analysis of the beginning postsecondary students study 2004. In Y. Kanno & L. Harklau (Eds.), *Linguistic minority students go to college: Preparation, access, and persistence* (pp. 110–129). New York: Routledge.

Oropeza, M. V., Varghese, M. M., & Kanno, Y. (2010). Linguistic minority students in higher education: Using, resisting, and negotiating multiple labels. *Equity & Excellence in Education, 43*(2), 216–231.

Testa, D., & Egan, R. (2014). Finding voice: The higher education experiences of students from diverse backgrounds. *Teaching in Higher Education, 19*(3), 229–241.

CASE 5.2
Fort Crimson Global Pathways

"'Are you sure you want to take the writing workshop for non-native English speakers? We can ask for an exemption, in light of your needs," advised Pamela.

In a meeting to determine Sooin's schedule for the spring semester at Fort Crimson's Institute for English Language Programs, Pamela meant well with her advice. "Even though this course is a requirement for all undergrads, I think we can make an exception in your case. After all, as an Education major, you will probably need more communication and hands-on classes. I just see that this course will be too laborious for you." Pamela has served as an academic advisor at Fort Crimson University for more than 15 years. A graduate herself, she is proud of all the university has to offer students in terms of extracurricular activities, from athletics to drama and other clubs. Although she has worked with a broad range of learners, she has never advised a blind student and her experience with international students is quite limited and historically unsuccessful. She had originally pushed back against the Fort Crimson Global Pathways program, which conditionally admitted students whose English language proficiency is not strong enough for direct admittance. However, she recently voiced at a college meeting that she was "pleasantly surprised by the success of the students as they come with very limited proficiency."

International students who are accepted in the Fort Crimson Global Pathways program take a year of English language classes and two sheltered courses within their discipline with accompanying tutoring. After Global Pathways scholars successfully complete this required year of intensive English classes, they can matriculate full-time during their sophomore year. Sooin was part of the university's first cohort of the Global Pathways program. She was admitted into the university's undergraduate education program. She hopes to return to Korea to become an elementary teacher and education advocate for students with disabilities.

"I think my university back home would like to see that I take this class as it is required for teachers back home. I have the technology to help me compose in a writing workshop. I believe I must take it," Sooin said during her meeting with Pamela. It was very hard for Sooin to disagree with the advice.

Although Sooin wrote the professor a month in advance of the writing workshop course to request the syllabus and access to the online course website, he never responded. Sean has been teaching Academic Writing for years to non-native English speakers at Fort Crimson's English Language Center. Although faculty receive monthly trainings and workshops, the topics always have to do with serving the language needs of typical students. Like most faculty in the English Language Center, Sean has never taken a course or attended a professional development workshop of strategies to support the needs of students with physical disabilities in the EAP classes. Upon receiving the physical syllabus from Sean on the first day of the course, Sooin was dismayed. She would not be able to read the syllabus along with the class without a digital version. Moreover, when someone read to her the course assignments listed on the syllabus (see Exhibit A), she became overwhelmed because there were no examples or an accompanying rubric to guide her success. In addition, there was no indication of where she could go to receive support services.

During the next class, Sean provided a list of transition words (see Exhibit B) that he wished for students to integrate into their writing, but again, he did not post it online nor did he email it to the students. It was merely posted on the board. Sooin, too shy to advocate for herself, asked a student to type and email the words to her.

Sean liked to incorporate readings into the course as a model for writers. Unfortunately, the book store said there was no ebook version of the required anthology of readings, and the physical copy was on back order. Sooin would have to wait an entire month to gain access to the text. When approached by Sean as to why she had not written the required one-page reflections on readings (see Exhibit B), she simply sighed and apologized for the delay. Internally, she was quite concerned about how the late submissions would impact her performance in the course.

The next class, Sean asked students to complete a journal reflection writing activity in response to a photograph displayed on the overhead projector. After about ten minutes of the free-write activity, Sean noticed that Sooin had not typed a word, while everyone else had completed at least a paragraph. Blushing, he realized when he looked at Sooin that he had not considered sending her the photo in advance.

Exhibit A: Course Assignments

Assignments

1. Weekly one-page papers. The response should "engage" the ideas of the specific essay and are due the day of class. Points will be deducted for late submissions.
2. Two essays (three to four pages) in two drafts. You will select the focus based on the assigned essays.
3. One research essay (five to seven pages) in two drafts. You will identify a researchable topic reflecting the themes/ideas explored in the specified essays.

Exhibit B: Transition Words List

To improve your writing, you need to make sure that your ideas, both in sentences and paragraphs, stick together or have coherence and that the gap between ideas is bridged smoothly. One way to do this is by using transitions—words or phrases or techniques that help bring two ideas together. Transitional words and phrases represent one way of gaining coherence. Certain words help continue an idea, indicate a shift of thought or contrast, or sum up a conclusion. Check this list of words to find those that will pull your sentences and paragraphs together.

For continuing a common line of reasoning:

consequently
clearly, then
furthermore
additionally
and
in addition
moreover
because
besides that
in the same way
following this further
also
pursuing this further
in the light of the... it is easy to see that

To change the line of reasoning (contrast):

however
on the other hand
but
yet
nevertheless
on the contrary

For opening a paragraph initially or for general use:

admittedly
assuredly
certainly
granted
no doubt
nobody denies
obviously
of course
to be sure
true
undoubtedly
unquestionably
generally speaking
in general
at this level
in this situation

Transitional chains, to use in separating sections of a paragraph that are arranged chronologically:

first... second... third...
generally... furthermore... finally
in the first place... also... lastly
in the first place... pursuing this further... finally
to be sure... additionally... lastly
in the first place... just in the same way... finally
basically... similarly... as well

I. Pre-Case Discussion Problem Sets

Complete the chart after reading the case.

Facts	
Opinions	
Assumptions	
Theories referred or connected to (if any)	
Ambiguous language	
Criteria you used in analyzing the case (e.g., emotional vs. rational)	
Emerging options	

Write a pre-case discussion decision paper. Include these points:

a. options for case resolution
b. criteria (a rational decision should always be made with a set of criteria)
c. analysis of options
d. recommendation (of the best choice among the options)
e. action plan

II. Case Discussion Questions

Big-Picture Analysis

Describe the context of the case:

- Fort Crimson Global Pathways program
- University and classroom context

Stakeholders

In small groups, assume the role of one of the case stakeholders. Write a statement/ dialogue expressing this person's or group's hypothetical feelings and perspectives. Be prepared to act out your roles to the large group.

- Pamela
- Sooin
- Sean

Surface Issues

What are the surface issues in this case? What is happening here from an untrained perspective? What underlying assumptions or beliefs feed into this perspective?

Deep Issues

Discuss the real issues in the case. Try to categorize them in terms of language teaching curriculum and instruction.

Evidence-Based Solutions

In groups, develop evidence-based solutions for each deep issue listed. Whenever possible, refer to a theory or principle of language learning and teaching to support your proposed solutions.

Teacher Thinking

In what ways does this case influence and/or reinforce your beliefs and dispositions as a teacher? Consult the Further Readings and Resources section to help with theoretically informed solutions.

III. Post-Case Problem Sets

Post-Case Analysis

A. Categorize what you learned as:
   - teacher knowledge and praxis (e.g., content knowledge, curricular knowledge, pedagogical content knowledge and application)
   - teacher thinking (e.g., beliefs, problem-solving strategies, prioritizing objectives, values, professional ethics, attitudes)

B. List:
   - learning objectives that you discovered in the case
   - potential learning outcomes
   - implications for your pedagogical practices

C. The post-case problem sets introduce reactions from various perspectives. These quotes are from others who have read the cases for educational and pedagogical purposes. Read all of the quotes and then choose two quotes about which to write a short response (put the quotes at the top of each response). Use these questions as a guide:
   - What is the message the speaker is trying to convey? If possible, also explain why you chose the quote.
   - What examples can you think of that connect to the themes presented?
   - Can you relate the quote to a class discussion or to something you have read or experienced?

Quotes

1. "The teacher should have responded sooner to the student and identified her needs in advance so that he would know how best to support her. It is always best to be proactive rather than reactive."
2. "This is not so much the fault of the teacher as it is of the university structure. Most faculty do not receive training or support on how to make content accessible to students with visual impairments or other disabilities."
3. "Although sentence starters and visuals are great supports, this case made me realize that even these accommodations need to be differentiated depending on the learners we serve. We should make no assumptions."
4. "It is not Sean's responsibility to provide the extra support services for Sooin. The university should have a team of support specialists who do this work."
5. "The advisor seems to have a very negative attitude about the global pathways program and lowered expectations for Sooin. As universities look to increase diversity and internationalize, there should be parallel trainings for staff to support their understanding and practice of diversity, equity, and inclusion."

D. Write a reflection describing a take-away from the case in terms of praxis. Make sure to develop an action plan to resolve the case. Consider these questions as guidelines:

- In what ways did the case discussion influence your thinking about the case?
- Did you change your original decision or did the discussion reaffirm your position?
- What points had you not considered prior to the case discussion?
- How might the information you gained from this case be applicable to your current instructional setting and/or future instructional settings?
- What did you learn?
- What are you inspired to learn more about?
- How did the themes discussed in class apply to your experience?

E. Discuss what theoretical basis there is for:
- the stakeholders' behaviors in the case.
- the solutions you proposed.

Further Reading and Resources

Anderson, C. (2003). Cutting through the jargon. In the Penrith Vision Support Team (Ed.), *Teaching a student who has a vision impairment: Implications and strategies for the classroom through experience of low vision and blindness.* NSW, Australia: Department School Education and Training.

Artiles, A., & Ortiz, A. (Eds.). (2002). *English language learners with special needs: Identification, placement, and instruction.* Washington, DC: Center for Applied Linguistics.

Baca, L. M., & Cervantes, H. T. (2004). *The bilingual special education interface* (4th ed.). Upper Saddle River, NY: Pearson.

Burgstahler, S., & Cory, R. (2010). *Universal design in higher education: From principles to practice.* Cambridge, MA: Harvard Education Press.

Hamayan, E., Marler, B., Sanchez-Lopez, C., & Damico, J. (2013). *Special education considerations for English language learners.* Philadelphia: Caslon.

Hodge, B. M., & Preston-Sabin, J. (1997). *Accommodations—or just good teaching? Strategies for teaching college students with disabilities.* Westport, CT: Praeger.

Kalyanpur, M., & Harry, B. (2012). *Cultural reciprocity in special education: Building family-professional relationships.* Baltimore: Brookes.

May, A. L., & Stone, C. A. (2010). Stereotypes of individuals with learning disabilities: Views of college students with and without learning disabilities. *Journal of Learning Disabilities, 43*(6), 483–499.

Sacks, S. Z. (1998). Educating students who have visual impairments with other disabilities: An overview. In S. Sacks & R.K. Silberman (Eds.), *Educating students who have visual impairments with other disabilities* (pp. 3–38). Baltimore: Brookes.

Scorgie, K., Kildal, L., & Wilgosh, L. (2010). Post-secondary students with disabilities: Issues related to empowerment and self-determination. *Developmental Disabilities Bulletin, 38,* 133–145.

Silver, P., Bourke, A., & Strehorn, K. C. (1998). Universal instruction design in higher education: An approach for inclusion. *Equity & Excellence in Education, 31*(2), 47–51.

CASE 5.3

Shoreham English Language Institute

At Shoreham English Language Institute, Mike teaches the Integrated Skills for Academic English Success course. The course expectations are to help broaden and develop students' English language proficiency for academic and professional purposes. This is an excerpt from the course description:

> This course fully employs the integrated skills approach to improving students' command of English for academic purposes. This course has been prepared for students who wish to improve their English language skills because they have serious academic aims. As the title suggests, the lessons cover current and enduring subject matter in important areas of academic life while expanding reading, writing, listening, and speaking skills. Students who complete this course are well on their way to dealing with the rigors of university courses. The course uses a content-based approach, with all of the readings stemming from journals, anthologies, high-level newspapers, or speeches by prominent national and global leaders. Student-centered exercises and activities require active participation and sharing in the learning process, and the activities are linguistically as well as intellectually challenging.

During the third week of class, following a homework reading assignment of the text, "The Abolition of Torture" by Andrew Sullivan, Mike asked students to participate in a fishbowl discussion (see Exhibit A) with this prompt: *Shouldn't we do anything to stop terrorist attacks, including using torture? Support your response with evidence.*

In "The Abolition of Torture," Sullivan objects to torture "under strictly curtailed conditions" as a violation and abandonment of U.S. constitutional principles and maintains this country's status as a defender of human rights; he supports the complete ban of torture.

Mike reminded students that he expected everyone to participate equally and that oral practice is essential. A seasoned teacher with more than 15 years in EAP, Mike has taught the Integrated Skills for Academic English Success at Shoreham English Language Institute for the last eight years. With a PhD in Linguistics, he wants to integrate the latest research-based strategies in his practice. However,

Mike looks critically and dismissively at theories such as critical pedagogy and culturally responsive teaching as he thinks that students needs to focus on the more important aspects of language gaps.

Based on latest research in promoting active oral participation, Mike included sentence starters to support the engagement of all learners (see Exhibit B). His class comprised 12 students from Latin America, Europe, Asia, and Africa. Some of his students were immigrant adult learners with intentions of improving their academic English for advanced college study or professional development, while other were international graduate students. For the logistics of the fishbowl discussion, Mike divided the class in half to form the inner and outer circles of the fishbowl discussion. The six students on the outside were expected to provide feedback on their peers' grammar, pronunciation, and discourse.

Esther, an immigrant student from Russia, made effective use of the sentence starters as she passionately shared her firm perspective about the use of torture. "Look what happened during 9/11. I am fan of torture and interrogation, especially with these suspicious Muslims." Although a few other students tried to oppose her racist and offensive position, she insisted that interrogation of any suspicious-looking Muslims was necessary. Fernanda, a Brazilian international student, rebuked this notion, "I am for the humane treatment to all people. One bad action no deserve another." Esther remarked, "I understand your idealistic view; quite frankly, I have lived here. I have lived events of 9/11 and mass murder by radical extremist Muslims. I think you are naïve to think the U.S. does not have right to defend herself. This country was founded by Christians. They have a right to protect themselves; this is no profiling. This is reality in our times."

Sitting in the room were two students: Sahara, a 40-year-old woman wearing a hijab, and Indrianti, a 25-year-old student from Indonesia. Sahara escaped civil war and torture and trauma as a refugee to the U.S. seven years ago. She hopes to improve her academic English skills so that she can enroll in a master's program in Public Policy. Her plans are to open her own nonprofit agency that provides educational training and services to Somali refugee teachers and parents. Indrianti, who was not wearing a hijab, joined the course as a pre-requisite to her enrollment into the MBA program at Shoreham University. Indrianti is a practicing Muslim. See Exhibit C for general country facts about Indonesia. This was her first month in the United States. For the first few weeks of the class, she had been extremely friendly and outgoing, although her written skills were stronger than her speaking and listening skills.

Sahara jumped into the conversation. "I lived the torture in Somalia. I experienced what is like to hear bullets rain behind the school as a primary school student," she said. "The terrorists, they want to scare us, to show their power. In the end, they succeed. But this is the way of ignorant tyrants. We cannot behave like them. This is why I escaped my country. This kind of thinking is equally as radical."

Esther persisted, "The U.S. has faced threats and the reality is it is from radical Muslims so if it were another religion perpetuating these crimes we would have the right to interrogate such a group. It is sad what happened to Japanese internment camps but sadly this is the reality our times. We have to take precautions."

The teacher remained silent and redirected the conversation to peer feedback on language. Esther's comments and the tension in the room were unaddressed.

When Sahara got home to her family, she described the situation: "I cannot believe the teacher allowed this kind of racist thinking to pervade the room. As a Muslim woman who escaped this kind of torture, I was mystified. I would not speak up because of my respect for his authority and the harmony of the group, but I do not feel comfortable returning to the class."

One week later, Sahara stopped showing up to the class. Mike could not understand the reason for this as Sahara expressed commitment and passion to improve her English skills to enroll in graduate study. He prided himself on being awarded annually the Excellence in Teaching Award so he knew he was using what he considered to be best practice in the field. He was also curious about Indrianti's withdrawal and disengagement from the class. To show his concern, he asked, "Is everything okay? Just checking in as you have been quiet and my expectation is for you to speak as much as possible so that you can develop your speaking proficiency. Practice makes perfect, remember!" Indrianti responded, "Everything is okay teacher. I am so sorry for my silence. I will try to do better."

Completely oblivious to her underlying reason for disengagement, Mike got up to erase the board and pack up his laptop.

Exhibit A: Fishbowl Discussion Guidelines

In a fishbowl discussion, some members of the class sit in an inner circle and respond to a question. These students will be considered the "fish" in the fishbowl. As they navigate through an eight-minute discussion, the other students (a.k.a. "humans observing the "fish") sit in an outer circle and are assigned by the instructors to observe either the syntactic, pronunciation, or discussion flow errors. At the end of the discussion, the students on the outside <u>must</u> each provide at least two pieces of constructive criticism to the students in the inner circle.

<u>Note:</u> As your instructor, my job is not to state whether your opinions are wrong or right, but rather to support your ability to orally defend your position. I wish to encourage free, expressive thinking in the class.

Exhibit B: Sentence Starters for Academic Conversation

- *I see what you mean, but. . . .*
- *That is an interesting point, however. . . .*
- *I see it somewhat differently. . . .*
- *That may be true, however. . . .*
- *I strongly agree. . . .*
- *I strongly disagree. . . .*
- *Yes, but on the other hand. . . .*

Exhibit C: Indonesia Country Facts

Indonesia has the largest Muslim population in the world with approximately 225 million Muslims. More than 87.2 percent of Indonesians are Muslim.

I. Pre-Case Discussion Problem Sets

Complete the chart after reading the case.

Facts	
Opinions	
Assumptions	
Theories referred or connected to (if any)	
Ambiguous language	
Criteria you used in analyzing the case (e.g., emotional vs. rational)	
Emerging options	

Write a pre-case discussion decision paper. Include these points:

a. options for case resolution
b. criteria (a rational decision should always be made with a set of criteria)
c. analysis of options
d. recommendation (of the best choice among the options)
e. action plan

II. Case Discussion Questions

Big-Picture Analysis

Describe the context of the case including:

- Shoreham English Language Institute
- Integrated Skills for Academic English Success course

Stakeholders

In small groups, assume the role of one of the case stakeholders. Write a statement/dialogue expressing this person's or group's hypothetical feelings and perspectives. Be prepared to act out your roles to the large group.

- Sahara
- Mike
- Esther
- Indrianti
- Other students in the class

Surface Issues

What are the surface issues in this case? What is happening here from an untrained perspective? What underlying assumptions or beliefs feed into this perspective?

Deep Issues

Discuss the real issues in the case. Try to categorize them in terms of language teaching curriculum and instruction.

Evidence-Based Solutions

In groups, develop evidence-based solutions for each deep issue listed. Whenever possible, refer to a theory or principle of language learning and teaching to support your proposed solutions.

Teacher Thinking

In what ways does this case influence and/or reinforce your beliefs and dispositions as a teacher? Consult the Further Readings and Resources section to help with theoretically informed solutions.

III. Post-Case Problem Sets

A. Categorize what you learned as:

- teacher knowledge and praxis (e.g., content knowledge, curricular knowledge, pedagogical content knowledge and application)
- teacher thinking (e.g., beliefs, problem-solving strategies, prioritizing objectives, values, professional ethics, attitudes)

B. List:

- learning objectives that you discovered in the case
- potential learning outcomes
- implications for pedagogical practices

C. The post-case problem sets introduce reactions from various perspectives. These quotes are from others who have read the cases for educational and pedagogical purposes. Read all of the quotes and then choose two quotes about which to write a short response (put the quotes at the top of each response). Use these questions as a guide:

- What is the message the speaker is trying to convey? If possible, also explain why you chose the quote.
- What examples can you think of that connect to the themes presented?
- Can you relate the quote to a class discussion or to something you have read or experienced?

Quotes

1. "The teacher did a great job integrating sentence starters and encouraging higher order thinking through contextualized learning. It is not is fault that adults do not know how to behave."
2. "Mike needs to learn how to navigate difficult conversations about race and religion. He did not intervene and this made the students of Muslim origin feel marginalized."
3. "The teacher showed no evidence of identifying learner's backgrounds and needs. Had he done so, this entire situation could have been avoided altogether."

D. Write a reflection describing a take-away from the case in terms of praxis. Make sure to develop an action plan to resolve the case. Consider these questions as guidelines:

- In what ways did the case discussion influence your thinking about the case?
- Did you change your original decision or did the discussion reaffirm your position?
- What points had you not considered prior to the case discussion?
- How might the information you gained from this case be applicable to your current instructional setting and/or future instructional settings?
- What did you learn?
- What are you inspired to learn more about?
- How did the themes discussed in class apply to your experience?

E. Discuss what theoretical basis there is for:

- the stakeholders' behavior in the case.
- the solutions you propose.

Further Reading and Resources

Boysen, G. A. (2012). Teacher and student perceptions of microaggressions in college classrooms. *College Teaching, 60*(3), 122–129.

Cheung, F., Ganote, C. M., & Souza, T.J. (2016). Microaggressions and microresistance: Supporting and empowering students. In *Faculty Focus special report: Diversity and inclusion in the college classroom* (pp.15–17). Madison, WI: Magna Publications.

Heron, M., & Webster, J. (2019). Scaffolding talk in EAP lessons: An examination of experienced teachers' practices. *Innovation in Language Learning and Teaching, 13*(4), 358–370. doi: 10.1080/17501229.2018.1466892

Hinkel, E. (2004). *In teaching academic ESL writing: Practical techniques in vocabulary and grammar.* New York: Routledge.

Hollins, E. R. (1996). *Culture in school learning: Revealing the deep meaning.* New York: Routledge.

Johns, T. F. (1981). Some problems of a world-wide profession. In J. McDonough & T. French (Eds.), *The ESP teacher: Role, development and prospects.* ELT Documents: 112. Oxford, England: ELT Publishing.

Jordan, R. R. (1997). *English for academic purposes: A guide and resource book for teachers.* Cambridge, England: Cambridge University Press.

McCarter, S., & Jakes, P. (2009) *Uncovering EAP: How to teach academic writing and reading.* Oxford, England: Macmillian.

Nagda, B.A., Gurin, P., Sorensen, N., & Zuniga, X. (2009). Evaluating intergroup dialogue: Engaging diversity for personal and social responsibility. *Diversity & Democracy, 12*(1), 4–6.

Obear, K. (2016). How to facilitate triggering situations. Online manuscript. Boston: Alliance for Change. Retrieved from www.alliance4change.com

Snow, M., & Brinton, D. (2020). *Content-based language instruction: What every ESL teacher needs to know.* Ann Arbor: University of Michigan Press.

Souza, T.J. (2016). Managing hot moments in the classroom: Concrete strategies for cooling down tension. In *Faculty Focus special report: Diversity and inclusion in the college classroom* (pp. 4–6). Madison, WI: Magna Publications.

Souza, T. J., Vizenor, N., Sherlip, D., & Raser, L. (2016). Transforming conflict in the classroom: Best practices for facilitating difficult dialogues and creating an inclusive communication climate. In P. M. Kellett & T. G. Matyok (Eds.), *Transforming conflict through communication: Personal to working relationships* (pp. 373–395). Lanham, MD: Lexington Books.

6

Applications

In our dynamic, globalized world, language learning has become a means to cross linguistic and cultural boundaries and to support integration and academic literacy to ensure equitable education opportunities and social justice. The 21st century language teacher's competencies should integrate a solid theoretical and pedagogical base along with cultural responsiveness, open-mindedness, contextual flexibility, and problem-solving orientations. With its emphasis on reflective practice and validating learners' experiences, case-based pedagogy is particularly attuned to the needs of language educators. It is designed to promote teachers' critical thinking by asking them to distinguish between facts and assumptions and surface and deep issues, as well as to critically analyze contextual factors and multiple perspectives to co-construct evidence-based solutions. Case-based pedagogy guides its practitioners toward creative, yet grounded, solutions to common issues in contemporary language classrooms, while simultaneously providing the lifelong professional value of collaboration in the field of language teaching and learning.

The distinguishing feature of this book is that it allows practitioners to read, analyze, and debate reflectively about carefully selected cases from authentic learning and teaching contexts that represent typical challenges. It provides current and aspiring language educators with the opportunity to develop an evidence-based, structured approach to thinking about and solving practical dilemmas.

The overarching themes that run through the cases include: communicating effectively with linguistically and culturally diverse families and fostering home-school connections; assessing learners' holistic needs (e.g., socioemotional, cultural, educational); distinguishing between learning disabilities and language-based issues; integrating inclusive and culturally response teaching strategies in diverse learning environments; differentiating teaching and assessment in multi-level classrooms; scaffolding reading, writing, listening, and speaking in second/foreign language classrooms; and supporting access to second/foreign language instruction for dually diagnosed learners (e.g., English learners with physical or cognitive disabilities). Even though this is not a finite list, it showcases the transformative potential of the case-based methodology in that it sensitizes practitioners to become acute observers and hones their ability to assess emerging challenges and develop an effective plan of action.

Among the many advantages of this case-based approach are: It is scalable and can be adapted to various educational settings; it reflects the complexity of the modern language learning classroom; it is attuned to the learning styles and needs of global citizens; it is engaging, empowering, and professionally rewarding for both the case facilitators and the participants; it offers a productive blend of theory and practice; and it is inclusive, yet personalized, and meaningful.

A possible extension of the method could be to assign the writing of the cases to the participants. We have occasionally used that format with participants who have more advanced formal training and teaching experiences. By harnessing the experiences of pre-service and in-service language teachers, cases generated by them could augment the scope of the issues under scrutiny and satisfy the learners' need for immediate application of knowledge. If that option were chosen, the outline that follows provides guidance to case writing.

Guide to Writing a Case

Step One: *Reflect and Write*

In a one-page journal reflection, describe in detail what you perceive to be one of the most significant instructional, professional, or programmatic dilemmas that you have experienced when teaching language learners.

Step Two: *Outline Key Concepts*

A well-written case must include a detailed explanation of these elements, which are usually presented in the form of "exhibits":

Topic	Details
The school context (mission statements, demographic information, sociocultural setting, etc.)	
The instructional program (curricular excerpts, program descriptions, or other relevant information about the curricular and learning environment)	
The classroom (classroom settings from physical environment to affective aspects of the setting, such as teachers' and students' attitudes)	

The characters (rich description of the key characters' backgrounds and quotes/conversations/ discourse that describe dilemma)	
The dilemma (plot of the situation)	

Step 3: *Drafting*

Use the outline to help guide your first draft writing of the case. The case should be written in the third person and should tell a story. You may include quotations from characters in the case, school mission statements, references to standards, or whatever you think will provide a comprehensive picture of the complexity of the issue. As a writer of the case, your view should be neutral; the case should have no assumptions, stated conclusions, or arguments. However, since these student case studies will be used for in-class case method discussions, it is important that you provide sufficient information upon which your colleagues will be able to base their arguments and conclusions when analyzing your case. For the purposes of professional confidentiality, it is important *not* to provide the real names of the subjects or school involved, so you need to substitute the real names with imaginary ones.

Step 4: *Peer Editing*

Exchange your case with a partner in class. Read his/her case and complete this rubric to discuss first draft strengths and areas in need of improvement.

Peer Editing Checklist	
1. Is the case written in third person and does it tell a story?	Y/N
2. Does the case include authentic information for analysis? (e.g., quotations from characters in the case, school mission statements, references to standards, or whatever you think will provide a comprehensive picture of the complexity of the issue.)	Y/N
3. Is the author's view neutral? Does the case have no stated conclusions or arguments?	Y/N
4. Does the case provide enough information in all categories to analyze in a class discussion?	Y/N
5. Does the case present a relevant and meaningful topic for class discussion?	Y/N
6. What are the case draft's strengths and weaknesses?	

Step 5: *Revise*

Taking your peer feedback into consideration, edit and revise a final draft of your case study.

The additional resources and online Commentary should also ensure a productive case discussion and set a model for successful future application of the case methodology. We wish you enjoyable and rewarding teacher training.